mlet

Nasing

Puddocks

Common

Vicarage

Church Green

Prophet Hill

Nasing wood

Nasing Lodge

Common

Epping Long Green

Hoods

Green Bridge

Wrights

Harolds Park

Hunters Hall

Peevels

Park

Boughtle

Copped

Giles

Bury

Gate Farm

Five miles from everywhere

The story of Nazeing, part 1.
From earliest times to 1914.

Two recognisable views of Nazeing in years gone by. Above is the main cross-roads in Lower Nazeing looking towards Middle Street at the time of the First World War. Below is the gate to Nazeingwood Common with the pound to the left and the King Harold's Head behind.

Five miles from everywhere

The story of Nazeing, part 1.
From earliest times to 1914.

David Pracy   John Garbutt   Colin Dauris

with

Russell Martin   Valerie Day   Doug Ball

"Nazing … is high and wide and five miles from everywhere." – Edward Hardingham, 1907

Nazeing History Workshop

2000

ISBN 0 9537135 0 4

Nazeing History Workshop Publication no. 4

Printed by St Edmundsbury Press, Bury St
Edmunds, Suffolk IP33 3TU

**Previous publications by members of
Nazeing History Workshop**

1. Not a better set in the country: the story
    of Nazeing Wood or Park 1778-1950.
    (David Pracy, 1995)

2. Nazeing Bury: the story of a house and its
    people. (John H. Gervis, 1997)

3. Nonconformity in Nazeing: a history of the
    Congregational Church 1795-1995.
    (Norman Bonnett and Paddy Hutchings,
    1999)

Contents

List of illustrations

Acknowledgements

Nazeing History Workshop was so named in order to encourage active participation by its members - a hope that has been fulfilled beyond all expectations. The authors would like to thank those without whose efforts this publication would have been impossible: Norman Bonnett, John Clark, Prudence Dauris, Desmond Day, John and Margaret Gervis, Cliff Gould, Peter Huggins, Paddy Hutchings, Liz Kenworthy, Pat Leach and the late Roy Leach, Irene Linnell and the late Robin Linnell, Tom Papworth, Michael and Shirley Roos, Brian Starling, and many others.

We would also like to thank:

Nazeing Parish Council, which made a most generous grant of £1,000 towards our publication costs and allowed us to reproduce pages from its early minute-books.

The Trustees of Nazeing Wood or Park, which also allowed us to reproduce pages from its minute-book.

Nazeingbury Residents' Association, which sadly was disbanded in 1998 and kindly donated £80. This helped to pay the Essex Record Office fee for reproducing the illustration of Nazeing Park on the back cover.

Peter and Enid Brent, John Graham, Arthur Hollow, Adelaide Starling and Elizabeth Wells - lifelong Nazeing residents whose parents and grandparents lived and worked in Nazeing before the First World War.

Shelagh Ball, Alan Church, Neville Cole, Brian Coleman, David Dent, Tina Dobrowolski, Joan Mansfield, Rachel Montgomerie-Charrington, Brian Murphy, the Hon. Harry Palmer, Russell Robertson, John Walker, and Josie Watson née Hampton for special help with illustrations and information.

The staff of the various record offices, archives and libraries, who sometimes came up with the right answer even before we had formulated the question.

Many illustrations in this book are photographs owned or taken by the authors and other members of Nazeing History Workshop. We also wish to acknowledge illustrations reproduced by courtesy of: The Ashmolean Museum (page 49), The Courtauld Institute (page 48), Essex Record Office (jacket, pages 54 and 68), The Mercers' Company (pages 96, 133, 137 and 138), Northamptonshire Record Office (pages 26, 80 and 81), The Paul Mellon Centre for Studies in British Art and the National Trust (page 67).

Every effort has been made to trace and seek permission from copyright holders. The authors will be glad to hear from anyone who has been inadvertently omitted.

PREFACE

"Pride in our birthplace, or village, town, or city of residence, is the inherent right of all people, and we have many reasons to be justly proud of our village, but these reasons may not be known to a considerable number of our readers." So wrote Alfred Perkins, under his pseudonym A. Sojourner, in the introduction to the series of articles on the history of Nazeing which he contributed to *Nazeing Parish Magazine* from 1929 to 1933. He seems to have been the first person to try to make people here aware of the history of their village. In a later article he admitted, that much more research could be done: "The more one digs into records relating to our village, the greater becomes the wonderment that no villager of antiquarian bent has hitherto undertaken to write, in sequence form, its not unimportant history. Perhaps these articles may be an incentive to that desirable end." In *Five miles from everywhere* we are attempting, seventy years on, the task which Perkins set.

It is debatable whether Nazeing's history is "not unimportant". The village features in no national history and is mentioned in only the more comprehensive county histories. Its story is not even unusual for, with a few changes, it could be that of many villages in England or elsewhere. It tells of how ordinary people came to live in the village, or left it, how they made a living, settled their disputes, and coped with difficulties and disasters. Yet for those who live or have lived in Nazeing, who know its landscape, its fields, and its buildings, and who are to any extent familiar with the names of local families, what happened in this one village is likely to be of special interest. To those people particularly this book is addressed.

When the authors began digging, as Perkins called it, they became surprised at how much information could be discovered. For this reason it was decided to publish in two volumes. The first deals with the period to the outbreak of the First World War, the second will cover the twentieth century.

We offer this history, not as a last word on the subject but in the hope that it will be a stimulus to others to delve further, in documents or on the ground. New evidence may refute, alter, confirm, or add to ideas which we have advanced. It is not too early to start, as there is always the danger that evidence will be lost by for example, the destruction of potential written sources or the development of land. In Nazeing one saddening break with the past has been that several houses which had retained their names for five or six centuries have had them changed, mostly since 1945. As many such losses are inadvertent, we hope to foster in our village a wider sense of its continuity and of our responsibility to preserve links with the past for the interest of future generations. If we succeed in this, we shall have achieved a worthwhile purpose.

NOTE

A glossary on page 183 gives notes on some places and events, as well as the meanings of some terms used in this book. At the end of the glossary are the values of currency, weights and measures. In the index we have included the dates of people and the addresses of houses to help identification.

"A most peculiar Common" – The junction of Common Road and Back Lane around 1900.

CHAPTER 1

"PEOPLE OF THE HEADLAND"

Early times to 1060

Landscape and early settlement

The main physical features of Nazeing were created long before the arrival of humans, who have only made minor changes by activities such as agriculture, disforestation, drainage, road making, and gravel extraction. The great landscape historian, W.G. Hoskins, has said "everything is older than we think" and so, to understand why and when there was settlement here, we need to study the physical characteristics of the area.

The most conspicuous features of the landscape are the steep slopes of Nazeingwood Common and Epping Long Green, the flat plain nearer the River Lea and the small hills between them. During the third glaciation of the Ice Age, about 200,000 years ago, the ice sheet which covered most of England moved the valley of the Thames southwards to its present line and formed the ridges on either side of the new course of the Lea. On the north and east side of the village are slopes formed by land movements and extreme changes in temperature, which left heavy deposits of London Clay. The gravel terrace in the Lea valley dates from the following interglacial period and the alluvial deposits there are from the last glaciation, when the river was much wider than it is now. The narrowing of the river left fertile silt in the Meads area, which probably attracted our ancestors who parcelled it out in strips for grazing. South of these were the Marshes, a boggy and therefore less valuable area which was nevertheless gradually drained and cleared of reeds and rushes. A brook which rises on Nazeingwood Common flows westward into the Lea, cutting Nazeing roughly in half. Into the brook run several tributaries, which in recent years have become much less obvious than they used to be. The London Clay was fertile but heavy and difficult to work, and therefore often the last to be occupied and the first to be abandoned. The whole Lea Valley region was covered in woods inhabited by wild animals; remains of mammoths, bears and deer have been found in Nazeing.

As little is known of Nazeing in early times, we can do little more than make educated guesses from the limited archaeological evidence and from comparisons with neighbouring areas. The first humans in Nazeing seem to have been hunter-gatherers who had arrived in Britain during the Mesolithic period, after the retreat of the ice. They certainly used sites at Broxbourne and Waltham Abbey around 6000 B.C. and they probably ranged throughout the Lea valley. There is a Neolithic site on the north side of Waltham Abbey but nothing definite from that period has been found any nearer. Nazeing is said to be near a prehistoric trackway from Chesham in Buckinghamshire to Marks Tey, the crossing-point of the Lea having been marked by a stone at Fishers Green. The earliest permanent settlement of which we know was in the first century B.C., when a Belgic farmstead was built in the area between Nazeing Bury and the river. It underwent enlargement and improvement before the Roman invasion of 43 A.D. but seems to have been abandoned in about 160, perhaps because a deteriorating economic situation led to the absorption of the farm into a larger estate. The land continued to be used for pasture. The existence of this farmstead was discovered almost by accident, so it is possible that there were other Belgic farms in Nazeing.

Nazeing was within the triangle linking London, Colchester, and Verulamium (St. Albans) which formed the heartland of early Roman Britain; there were significant Roman settlements at Waltham and Harlow. It is therefore likely that the riverside farm was not the only Roman presence in Nazeing and various speculative suggestions have been made about roads and other remains, although firm evidence is almost entirely lacking. In the 1930s, for example, a collection of pottery, consisting of two platters and two bowls from about 50 A.D. was found in Nazeing. Regrettably, details of exactly where they were found and even the potsherds themselves have been lost.

Before leaving the Romans we should dispose of the romantic but unfounded tradition that Queen Boudicca fought them in a battle on Nazeing Common. There is little doubt about the basic facts. When in 61 A.D. the military governor, Paulinus Suetonius, went to quell a revolt in Wales, Boudicca was queen of the Iceni, a British tribe whose territory covered much of Essex. She led a rebellion in which the Iceni destroyed Colchester, London, and Verulamium but then Paulinus returned and defeated her and the Iceni in a pitched battle. The site of this has never been located precisely, but it is almost certain that Boudicca confronted Paulinus in the Midlands. There are three reasons why it is improbable that a battle was fought in Nazeing: first, to have doubled back across the Lea is an unlikely strategy; secondly, Nazeing Common does not fit the site of the battle as described by Tacitus, the almost contemporary historian; thirdly, it has never yielded a single piece of first-century military hardware. The story of this great battle and another story, that she fought an earlier, bloodless skirmish in Nazeing, seem to be an extension of a myth which was first recorded in 1740, almost 1,700 years after the events it purported to describe. It claims, equally improbably, that Boudicca had fortified the earthworks at Ambersbury Banks in Epping Forest and squeezed some 120,000 people inside them.

The early Saxons and the naming of the village

Early in the fifth century the Roman army withdrew from Britain, and gradually the country was conquered by Angles, Saxons, and Jutes invading from northern Europe. In heavily wooded areas like west Essex, the settlers usually travelled by boat, so it is likely that they arrived in Nazeing via the River Lea. Place names can relate to their topographical character or the type of settlement, and Nazeing contains both these elements. The Old English word *næss,* or naze, is related to our word nose and refers to a spur or headland, while the suffix *-ing* means "the dwellers at", so the name can be translated as "People of the Headland". The Saxons first established compact settlements called hams; more scattered communities with names ending in *ing* followed a generation or two later. Waltham, the place in the wood, was probably settled by 600 A.D, which would suggest a date some time in the seventh century for its neighbour, Nazeing. Until recently the area around Nazeing Primary School was known as the Ham fields, and it is possible that their name recalls the site of the first settlement in Nazeing.

The headland which gave the village its name is often identified as the hill on which All Saints' Church is situated but all the evidence of early settlement comes from nearer the river. Further, such a usage does not fit with the normal Saxon one. Just as the Inuit (Eskimo) people have many words for snow, so the Saxons had a keen eye for variations in the landscape and their words for different types of sloping land express subtle differences. The ancient names Hoe Lane and Back Lane suggest that they may have referred to this feature as the *hoo* (Old English for heel, and used to describe a spur of land) or the *bæck* (OE for back, meaning a ridge). A naze was specifically a promontory of dry ground jutting into a sea, marsh, or river valley, and so Nazeing is more likely to have taken its name from a conspicuous feature which projected into the Lea, which was then much wider than it is today. Of the three pieces of high land nearest the river, Langridge (long ridge) and Perry Hill (peartree hill) both have Old English names which refer to the sloping nature of the ground but do not fit etymologically. Another possible candidate is the L-shaped feature in the area of present-day Maplecroft Lane which dominates the river valley.

W.G. Hoskins identifies three types of English village, surrounding a village green, along a street, and fragmented. His description of the last summarises how Nazeing was probably settled:

> ... where the houses are dotted about singly or in pairs, and joined together by a network of lanes or paths, we shall probably be right in seeing them as the result of individual squatting on the common pasture or in a clearing in thickly wooded country. Such squatters had no concerted plan and no leader with a small community around him, as in those numerous early villages the name of which embodies some Old English personal name. They acted individually and built wherever they had cleared a sufficient space, though always in close proximity to their neighbours. They were not building isolated farmsteads in the depths of the woods, but a loosely-framed village covering a considerable area. ...

Some village names suggest such clearings: Burmans or Brimmers (Bumbles) Green, Sedge Green, Long Green, Leonards Green, and Church Green (the Betts Lane Triangle).

Almost all the archaeological evidence so far discovered of the Saxon presence in Nazeing, however, comes from nearer the river. In 1934, for example, a local nurseryman was removing topsoil for foundations at Hainault Nursery not far from Carthagena Lock. Only two feet below the surface he found twenty human skeletons which were said to have been "all of them nearly seven foot tall ... with perfect teeth" and "decently buried ... in a sort of pattern". M. L. Tildesley, Human Osteological Curator of the Royal College of Surgeons, suggested that they were Christian burials from the ninth century or earlier, with the skeletons fully extended and heads to the west.

In 1972, on a spoil heap from gravel workings between the end of Green Lane and Kings Weir, Bill Dorset found a hoard of seventeen Saxon implements. They probably dated from the seventh or eighth century and had perhaps been dropped from a boat to the bed of the old River Lea. Carole Morris of Cambridge University stated that they were a metal worker's raw material and some tools of his trade, and declared that they were "an important addition to knowledge of artefacts of the early medieval period ... objects which are as yet unparalleled in England at this period ..."

The Nunnery

To the west of Nursery Road there is a lake which now forms part of the Lea Valley Park. One may be forgiven for not realising that it was the scene of the most significant archaeological find in the history of the village. In 1975-6 a major dig revealed a large Saxon site with two churches and a burial ground containing almost 200 graves.

In the summer of 1975 Redland Gravel had begun removing top soil in the fields called Blacklands. John Payne, a resident in Nursery Road, was exercising his dog one evening on some of the ground from which the top soil had been removed. He noticed a long black streak in the ground and discovered that it contained pieces of pottery in what was later shown to be a silted ditch. He knew of the archaeological finds made nearby in 1934 and was put in touch with Peter Huggins of the Waltham Abbey Historical Society. With the agreement of Redland, a full-scale dig was organised under the leadership of Mr Huggins, taking place mostly at weekends throughout the following twelve months.

A view of the gravel workings and the excavation of the Nunnery site.

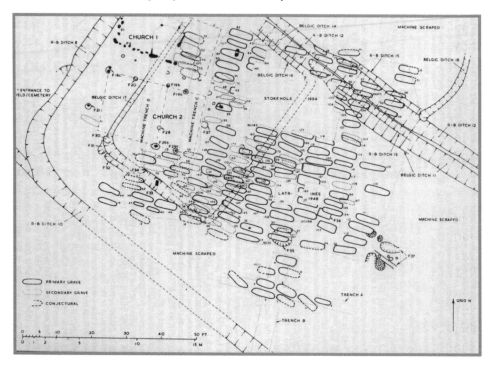

A plan of the Middle-Saxon Cemetery in Nazeing meads superimposed on earlier features.

The dig revealed ditches and postholes, indicating that there had been two wooden churches on the site. One is dated from *c*.700, the other from *c*.800; since their foundations did not overlap, they could have been in use at the same time. The earlier church showed the burials of two females aged fifty or over in front of where the altar would have been, a position normally expected for the founders of a religious house. Further study, including carbon 14 dating for one of these skeletons, provided a date range of *c*.660 to *c*.720 whereas another skeleton from elsewhere in the graveyard was dated to *c*.760 to *c*.870.

Detailed analysis of those skeletal remains from which the sex could be determined indicated that there was an exceptionally high proportion of females and that the divergence in build of the females and males was spectacular. One male aged approximately 50, who had suffered two broken hips and a broken left forearm, could not have reached such an age without a great deal of help. Another male of between 35 and 45 had a large and robust skeleton but he had fatigue fractures of both feet, and so could have been a pilgrim, ploughman, carter, or vagabond. Scurvy and rickets were absent, indicating a high level of nutrition. Dental studies showed far greater tooth wear in the males, suggesting either that they had a diet very different from that of the females or that they had not lived the main part of their lives on the site. For a middle Saxon community the balance between the sexes was most unusual; the extreme old age of its members and the degree of caring for the sick suggested a hospice run by a religious order of nuns. The better nourished women were the nuns, who at that time all came from royal or noble families, whereas the men and the other women were either invalids dying in their care or local people who worked for them.

A few years after the dig, the main findings of the report were confirmed by remarkable documentary evidence found in the library of Hatfield House, where a sixteenth century manuscript included a copy of two foundation charters which record the endowment between 693 and 709 of a House of God. The seventh century had seen the introduction of Christianity to the Kingdom of Essex, first by St. Mellitus for a brief period, and later by St. Cedd, who landed at Bradwell in 654. The charters were granted by King Suebred to a person called on the manuscript Fymme, a name which may have been corrupted in the course of copying. It is likely that Fymme was a close female relative of the king and that the endowment was a nunnery where she would have presided as the first abbess. If so, one of the two primary skeletons was almost certainly hers. Included in Suebred's grant were forty *manentes* (about 5,000 acres) of land with the fields, woods, meadows, pastures, and fisheries appertaining to it, a considerable estate which included Nazeing, together with Holyfield and part of Roydon. (See map on page 27.)

The Later Saxons and the Danes

It seems likely that the nuns carried on their work for about two hundred years until, in the course of a major invasion towards the end of the ninth century, pagan Danes destroyed the nunnery. The loss would have been very serious locally, as small religious houses were mainly responsible for pastoral care in the countryside and were the only hospices. The destruction would not, however, have been absolute, because the nunnery would probably have had stock and even arable land which needed labourers. When it closed the farming associated with it could have continued, perhaps after an interval, so that the land came to form the Lower Town manor, which certainly existed by the middle of the eleventh century.

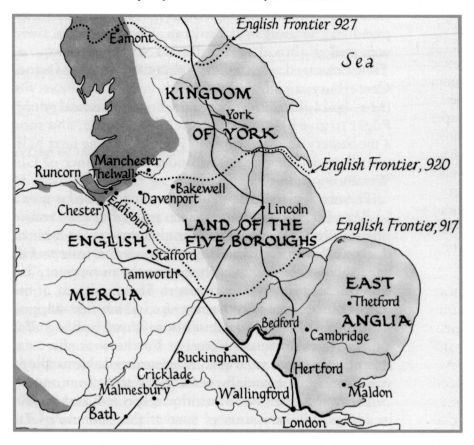

The Danelaw covered most of eastern England.

The Kingdom of Essex had extended well into Hertfordshire but, under the Treaty of Wedmore in 878, present-day Essex came under the Danelaw. The River Lea was established as part of the boundary between the Saxons and the Danes, so putting Nazeing on the frontier. After a few years the Danes broke the treaty and moved up the Lea, first pillaging Ware and Hertford and then establishing a fortified base some twenty miles above London. This provoked King Alfred to take vigorous counter-measures, which are described by Alfred's contemporary and biographer Asser and quoted in the Anglo-Saxon Chronicle. In the autumn of 895 the king camped close to the Viking stronghold, to protect the farmers at harvest, ensuring that the Danes could not interfere with them. Making a personal reconnaissance on horseback, the king found a spot where he could breach the riverbank to create new channels and drain the upper reaches, thus making them unnavigable. The Danes at Ware realised that their ships were trapped and so they abandoned them and went raiding as far as the river Severn. They camped there for the winter before dispersing. It is not known precisely where the king breached the bank, but one strong possibility is Kings Weir, once called Kings Breach.

Little is known of Nazeing during the tenth century and the first half of the

Alfred the Great, the first king of all England. He breached the banks of the Lea so that the boats of the Danes were marooned in Ware. Kings Weir in Nazeing was formerly called Kings Breach and may be the site of this incident.

eleventh so that the following suggestions, though plausible, can only be speculative. The destruction of the nunnery and the establishment of the frontier on the river probably prompted the population there to cross to the English side or to retreat to the comparative safety of the existing forest clearings. This was the period when the manorial system was developing and King Alfred would have been well aware of the strategic importance of Nazeing. He may therefore have authorised or even ordered the creation of a manor at Upper Town, centred on the area of All Saints' Church and Church Green, and probably including Roydon Hamlet. This would explain why the church, once at the heart of a manor, is now on the very edge of a parish, after a change to the manorial and parish boundaries. There could well have been a small wooden church at the Upper Town before Alfred's time, perhaps established in the seventh century on the site of an ancient holy place by followers of St. Cedd. If not, a church replacing the one at the nunnery could then have been built to serve the new manor house.

Waltham Hundred, like Essex, had comprised land on either side of the Lea but became divided by the Treaty of Wedmore. Nazeing therefore came to be one of only four well-separated parishes in a Half-Hundred, the others being Waltham, Chingford, and Epping. It is very likely that, while the threat of attack by the Danes remained, people moved away from the border area so that the parishes in the half-hundred were not just well separated but depopulated. Alfred's son Edward the Elder recaptured Essex from the Danes and a succession of strong English kings through most of the tenth century ensured a more peaceful period. This would have encouraged gradual resettlement and probably led to the establishment of a second manor, comprising Lower Nazeing and a small part of Epping. By the time of King Canute (1016-1035) the village had probably a hundred or so inhabitants, who would have had hard lives. They would have lived in simple wooden dwellings and have worked the land all year round. Probably they developed a sense of local identity in response to population growth and the need to husband resources. The carefully managed riverside meadowland was divided into strips on which each tenant grew hay. After mowing in June it was opened up for common grazing until autumn. Areas of unimproved common land would have been open to the animals, which were vital as beasts of draft and of burden, and as producers of manure.

It was during Canute's reign that lands near the river in Nazeing were given to his standard-bearer, Tovi (or Tofig). In about 1035 a figure of Christ on the Cross was discovered at Montacute in Somerset and brought by Tovi to Waltham. It was housed in the church which he caused to be rebuilt and dedicated to the Holy Cross. The cross from Montacute remained as an object of veneration until it disappeared at the Dissolution, five centuries later. Thus Waltham came to the notice of Earl Harold of Wessex, soon to become the most powerful man in England. This was to have a great effect on Waltham, and on Nazeing.

The death of King Harold at Hastings in 1066. From the Bayeux Tapestry.

CHAPTER 2

"HOLY CROSS HAS ALWAYS HELD NAZEING"

From Harold II to Henry VIII, 1060 to 1547

An event of 1060 was to affect Nazeing for the following four hundred and eighty years, a period longer than from its end to the present day. This was the foundation nearby of a religious house which was to become the centre of one of the most successful economic enterprises of mediaeval England. From this period there are some direct sources but to a considerable extent, we have to make inferences. These are from the local topography and from what we know was happening in England generally, and in this area particularly.

Following the death of Tovi the church at Waltham came into the possession of Harold Godwineson, Earl of Wessex, the most powerful man in England and later King Harold II. He converted it into a college of a dean and twelve secular canons, all literate men. The small stone church was replaced by a much grander one, which was consecrated on 3rd May 1060, appropriately on the Feast of the Invention (the finding) of the True Cross. To the manors with which the church was endowed already, Harold added twelve more, including Nazeing and its near neighbours, Netteswell and Wormley.

The Domesday Survey

A charter of Edward the Confessor confirmed the boundary of the estate in Nazeing, making it the part of the village north of the brook, which includes the Old Town and the parish church. The Great Survey of England of 1086, recorded in Domesday Book, found that the canons of the Church of the Holy Cross at Waltham had always held that manor. That meant both in the time of King Edward (before 1066) and currently. The land farmed by the canons was reckoned at five hides, as was that farmed by their tenants (a hide being about 120 acres). Both areas were described as one and a half ploughs; a plough team was usually eight oxen. A man holding ten to eighteen acres, known as a bovate or oxgang, had to contribute one ox to the co-operative team. In addition there was woodland which could support fifty pigs, and thirteen acres of meadow and half a fishery, probably in Nazeing Meads.

Nafingā sẽp ten& Scã crux . p . v . hid . Tc̃ . i . cař in dn̄io . m̊ . i . 7 dii̇m . Tc̃ . i . cař hom . m̊ . i . 7 . d . Sẽp . v . uilt . m̊ . ii . bor . Tc̃ . ii . feř . m̊ null . Silu̇ . l . por . .xiii . ac̃ . p̊ti . dim pilc̃ . i . ř . iiii . an̄ . x . por . Tc̃ . ual . xl . fot . m̊ lx .

"Holy Cross has always held Nazeing." A transcription of the Domesday Book's entry for the Upper Town Manor. There is a separate entry for the Lower Town manor held by Ranulf.

The other principal manor was south of the brook and was three quarters in Nazeing and one quarter in Epping. Its area was four and a half hides less fifteen acres, as well as woodland which could support a hundred pigs, fifty-four acres of meadow, and a mill on the Lea, which had ceased working by 1086. The lord of this manor's area was of a size to provide two plough teams, the villeins' to provide three. Before 1066 the manor was held by two freemen but after the Conquest it came to Ranulf, brother of Ilger, who held it in demesne, which meant for his own use. Ranulf was a prominent, and seemingly not over scrupulous, royal official, holding land in Parndon, Harlow, North Weald, and elsewhere in Essex, as well as in other counties. To his land in Nazeing another hide had been added; it had been held by a freeman in 1066 and was still held by a freeman in 1086. We can only guess where this piece of land was. In addition Ranulf had taken a virgate (30 acres) of land from the canons. A separate one hide equivalent to one plough, at the north of the parish, was held by Odo from Ranulf.

According to a document of 1765, the boundary between the Upper Town and the Lower Town of Nazeing lay for much of its length along the brook which "rises at the top of the Common". The document adds that the "Lands in Upper Town descend to the Youngest Son, the lands in Lower Town to the Eldest Son." This offers strong confirmation that the manorial boundary was early. Descent to the youngest son was known as Borough English, a rural custom widespread in villein tenure. Perhaps it was the Norman Ranulf who introduced Borough French, descent to the eldest son, to the southern manor.

The Great Survey recorded the working population, with changes in status over the twenty years after the conquest. On the canons' manor there were always five villeins (nowadays sometimes translated as villagers) but the two serfs of 1066 had become, or been succeeded by, two bordars. Villeins had land associated with the *villa*, bordars had usually less land, probably towards the edge of the village, and serfs had practically none. On many manors serfs were employed as the lord's beekeepers, haywards, swineherds, woodwards, etc.

The manor held by Ranulf in demesne had eleven villeins and three serfs in 1066 but seven villeins and nine bordars in 1086, while on the hide held by the freeman the number of bordars had increased from two to three. The manor held by Odo had just one villein and three bordars at the time of the survey. If we assume that all the workers on Ranulf's manor lived in Nazeing and that the three freemen of 1066 and the one of 1086 lived on their land, the total population recorded went up from twenty-six to thirty-one, or thirty-two if Ranulf had a resident reeve. The total population, including dependants, was therefore about a hundred and forty-five. The term "dependants" is used advisedly, as only infants and the bedridden did not work.

Although the Domesday survey gives a picture of Nazeing more detailed than any recorded for hundreds of years, from our point of view it has unfortunate omissions. Among these are that it made no mention of boundaries between manors or where buildings were. Therefore we are left to speculate about where the people dwelt, using what other evidence we have. Probably the seven families who worked on the Upper Town manor lived close to the junction of Betts Lane and Back Lane, where the layout of the roads indicates early Saxon settlement. As the sixteen families working on the Lower Town manor would have lived close to one another, then their hamlet was probably in Middle Street, street being the name which the Saxons gave to the principal thoroughfares in their settlements. There seem to be two likely positions for this hamlet, which may have been at one or both of them.

One is in the Perry Hill to Old House Lane area, which is close to the brook for water and had good routes to all parts of the manor, *via* Cemetery Lane and along Middle Street. In that area is a cluster of old houses which are, almost certainly, on the sites of much older dwellings. They are Smalldrinks, Shadwalkers, Ninnings, Perry Hill Farm, the Old House, and Mansion House, which may possibly recall the position of the manor house of the Lower Town. Mansion and manor have the same meaning. As the word "manor" came into English only in the fourteenth century, perhaps the name "Mansion House" continued from former days, though there seems to be no record of it before 1800.

"A Short description of the Boundary bet[ween] the Upper Town and Lower Town of Nazeing – 3rd August 1765" copied into the Manorial Records in 1816. It states towards the bottom "The Lands in Upper Town descend to the Youngest Son … in Lower Town to the Eldest Son" – evidence that Nazeing was split between two manors from the eleventh century.

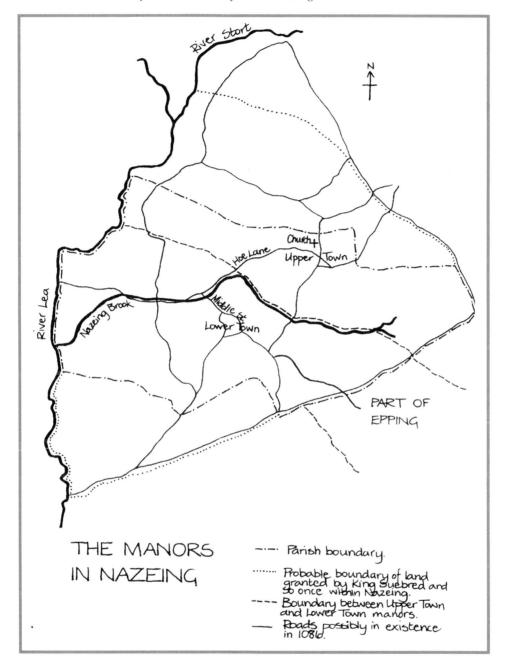

THE MANORS
IN NAZEING

–·– Parish boundary.

········ Probable boundary of land granted by King Suebred and so once within Nazeing.

– – – Boundary between Upper Town and Lower Town manors.

—— Roads possibly in existence in 1086.

The two manors of Nazeing, Upper Town and Lower Town

The other possible site for the original houses of the manor is further east along Middle Street where The Poplars, The White House, Curtis Farm, Goodalls, Motts (now Walnut Tree Cottages), Bentons, and

Sturtsbury are on ancient sites. From this part, opposite Goodalls, ran Church Lane, across to the corner of Back Lane and on, forming a direct route to the church. Another track ran beside where Orchard Cottage is now, continuing into Belchers Lane and on, beside Copy Wood, to the part of the manor in Epping. It is quite possible, however, that both areas on Middle Street were occupied by 1086.

The cultivated land would have been within easy reach of the houses on each of the two manors and was probably in open fields. Grazing would have been close by in winter and near the river Lea in summer. The requirement for grazing was not great, as the animals recorded in 1086, including those on the Epping part of Ranulf's manor, were one cob (a thick, strong pony), eight cattle, thirty-four pigs, and forty-one sheep.

Ranulf was alive in 1094 and probably in 1097 but seems to have died soon afterwards. Probably because he had no heirs, his honour escheated to the Crown and was broken up by fresh grants, the details of which are obscure. The land held of him by Odo seems to have become joined to that of Nether Hall, in Roydon. There is no doubt, however, that most of Ranulf's demesne lands in Nazeing were acquired by the canons of Waltham during the twelfth century. They may have come to Waltham through the Clares, one of the most powerful families in England from the Conquest until Bannockburn, or their under tenants, as did Stanstead Abbots. Part may have come through the Crown.

The founding of the Augustinian Abbey

In 1177 Henry II had obtained the Pope's permission to dissolve the college of secular canons at Waltham, who were claimed to be causing scandal by their irreligious and worldly lives, possibly just because they were married when clergy marriage had gone out of fashion. He founded a college of regular canons, who followed the rule of St. Augustine of Hippo, and so came to be known as Augustinian (or Austin) Canons. It was one of three monasteries founded by Henry as part of his penance for the murder of Thomas Becket. The buildings covered over ten acres, with the church being more than 400 feet long, four times as long as the part which remains today, and having two central towers, each with transepts 140 feet across. It was under construction for over half a century and became one of the most magnificent Norman buildings in the south of England. By his charter Henry gave to the canons title to two scrutlands in Nazeing with the church and all appurtances and the tithes of

Langridge. Each scrutland, land to supply the canons with clothing and from which the name of the house Cutlands is said to be derived, was two and a half hides. These made up the five hides which had been held by the Secular Canons in 1086. In 1189 Richard I granted to the abbey 160 acres in Nazeing, together with arable lands elsewhere. The canons' manor of Nazeing, thus enlarged to take in almost the whole parish, was retained by them until the Dissolution.

Between 1187 and 1189 Abbot Walter de Gant and the canons were inducted into the church and given possession by the Archdeacon of Essex, Robert Banastre. He confirmed the grant by the Pope of the advowson (the right to appoint to the living) of the church at Nazeing to the abbot and canons of Waltham. In December 1189 Richard I confirmed the canons' permission to appropriate the rectory to increase their income. A vicarage was not ordained until 1254, so it seems that for sixty-five years the canons served Nazeing on a casual basis. The names of the vicars from 1371 are recorded on a board in All Saints' church, where there is also a reference to William the Clerk who, in 1164,

witnessed a grant of land in Amwell. Although there is no mention of a church in Nazeing before the present building was started, from inferences and from the number of inhabitants, it seems that there had been a church building well before the Conquest and that the suggestion that the church in Nazeing is a daughter of that in Waltham is incorrect. The Normans, like many conquerors, tended to demolish even sound structures and to rebuild, expunging any record of what was there before. Therefore the present nave almost certainly replaced an earlier church when it was built a little before or after 1177, probably with a small chancel which was replaced in the fifteenth century.

Henry III was perhaps the most expensive guest to please when he visited Waltham Abbey.

Waltham Abbey enjoyed the privilege of exemption from control by the bishop and its abbots sat in parliament from the late thirteenth century. It was much favoured by kings, from Henry II to Henry VIII, as a hostelry. Henry III was perhaps the most expensive to please, as his feasts, described by Oliver Rackham, were among the greatest dinners

The "B" mark surmounted by a crown was used for cattle from Nazeing and Roydon grazing in the Forest of Waltham.

that these islands have known. Part of the attraction of Waltham was the hunting, as the abbey stood at the entrance to Waltham Forest from the Old North Road (Ermine Street). In Western Europe *forest* had come to mean land on which deer were protected by special bye-laws, with the word and the laws having been introduced to England by William the Conqueror. By 1215 there were 143 forests in England, most of them royal. *Magna Carta* forbade the creation of more. The legal boundary of Waltham Forest enclosed 60,000 acres in 1641, when the northern boundary was just beyond Roydon Hamlet and Broadley Common; earlier it was further north, probably including all of Roydon. Three quarters of the forest was ordinary Essex countryside, farms, hamlets, small woods, and parks. It included the town at Waltham, as well as the densely wooded area of the present Epping Forest, which at 6,000 acres is not much smaller now than it was when Henry I declared it. Multiplying forests was a way in which the king oppressed the nobility and, indirectly, the local population, as he kept his deer on their land. Deer can have been no more popular in Nazeing then than they are with its farmers today.

From later evidence we may deduce how the land in Nazeing was used at this time. The villeins and the lord of the manor had strips distributed over the open arable fields. As the population increased, smaller corn fields, at least some of them hedged, were taken into cultivation. In Nazeing Mead the villeins had strips which were cut for hay. These summer "leases", running down to the river Lea, existed until the enclosures in the middle of the nineteenth century. Cows grazed on the mead in the autumn, on the arable fields from harvest to ploughing (in the late winter), and on the waste, the area round the village, at other seasons. As the waste was within the forest, where cattle from the different villages mingled, at some time a system of marks was introduced. The mark for Nazeing cattle, including those from Roydon Hamlet, was a "B" surmounted by a crown.

Many field-names shown on nineteenth-century village surveys describe the physical appearance of the fields or how they may once have been used, thus revealing something of the landscape and economy of the village. Some are more modern but many date back to the mediaeval period. Hyde Mead, now a road name, was once a much larger area, of some 120 acres, which would have been enough to support a family. Seed Coope is a variant of an Essex dialect word meaning flat-topped hill and was the name of a field at Perry Hill. Buttfield, at Brewitts Farm, was probably used for archery practice. The Riddens, fields that lie beside Nazeing Long Green, take their name from an old English word related to modern "riddance" and refer to an area of cleared woodland. Nattox Mead, part of Nazeing Bury Farm, was an isolated piece of cultivable land in a swampy area. Nearby Blacklands was named from the dark soil where in the 1970s, significant archaeological remains were discovered. At Darmers, Napsies was sloping and Breechers was originally a newly broken piece of land. Clapgate Field at Langridge was probably infested with rabbit burrows. Cains Hill may well have been an infertile field, fancifully named after the biblical Cain who, as a punishment for the murder of his brother Abel, was told by God that "When thou tillest the ground it shall not henceforth yield unto thee her strength." Great and Little Football Fields would have been used for an early form of the game; Little Football Field has been devoted to recreational purposes for at least two centuries and perhaps more, so it is probably no coincidence that it is the field where Nazeing Football Club plays today. Several small areas called Oziers were to be found near the River Lea and Nazeing Brook and indicate coppiced willows used for basket making. The Slipe and various fields called Hoppits were small enclosures. Burnt Barn Field suggests some minor disaster, the details of which are lost. Brick Field, Chalk Field, Gravel Pits, Great Hogs Cote and Little Hogs Cote, Dove Croft, Oxhouse Field and Cowhouse Field all reveal what the fields were used for. Pease Ditch, Clover Field, Bushey Field, Damson Mead, Bramble Croft, Maple Croft, Thornlands, Shrubbery, Barley Field, Turnip Field, Long Bean Field, and Little Bean Field suggest the prevailing crop (or weed). Horse Nails was called after Thomas Horsnail who occupied it until about 1750. Owlets Hatch is a delightful field name, though its exact significance is unknown. It may be derived from the Waylett family who lived in Nazeing in the 17th century or even from William Aylid or Ayleth who in 1271 leased the Nazeing fishery.

The Wood or Park in Nazeing, a booming economy

Partly because of royal patronage, the abbey at Waltham became prosperous. One result of this was that the abbot and canons sought to have the current status symbol, a park. These were not hunting preserves but areas in which deer were kept to ensure a plentiful supply of venison. They began to be enclosed in the eleventh century and multiplied in the twelfth, doubtless because of the introduction of fallow deer, which are easier to keep within a confined space than native species. All modish earls, bishops, and monasteries aspired to one or more parks. So, in 1225, the abbot and canons of Waltham received a licence from the Earl of Pembroke, acting on behalf of Henry III, to empark their woods at Nazeing and Epping. It was stipulated that the park had to be enclosed by a little ditch and a low hedge so that the beasts of the chase might go in and out. What these beasts were, if they could clear the hedge while the fallow deer could not, we are not certain. In 1254 permission was given to repair the hedges and ditches and in 1286 to deepen the ditch and to raise the hedge so that the king's deer, passing through the forests of Waltham and Wintreye (a small part of which survives as Wintry Wood, north-east of Epping), might no longer seek refuge in the park. So it became excluded from the forest. There were to be two new gates, one towards Roydon called Lord's Hatch, probably Harknett's Gate now, and one towards Epping called Abbot's Hatch, probably to the north of Copy Wood.

In 1285 or just before the men of Roydon, feeling aggrieved, caused considerable havoc by tearing down the park fences. It is probable that they were from Roydon Hamlet and that they were trying to assert a grazing right predating the present line of the parish boundary. It was stated at an inquisition that indeed in the past the men of Roydon had to some extent intercommoned with those of Nazeing. In spite of that, it was decided that only the inhabitants of Nazeing had rights of common in the park and so the lord of Roydon, Robert Fitzwalter, renounced the right. From this episode it seems that the position of Harknett's Gate, separating Broadley Common from Nazeing, must have been well established by 1285.

For economy of fencing or hedging the usual shape of parks was

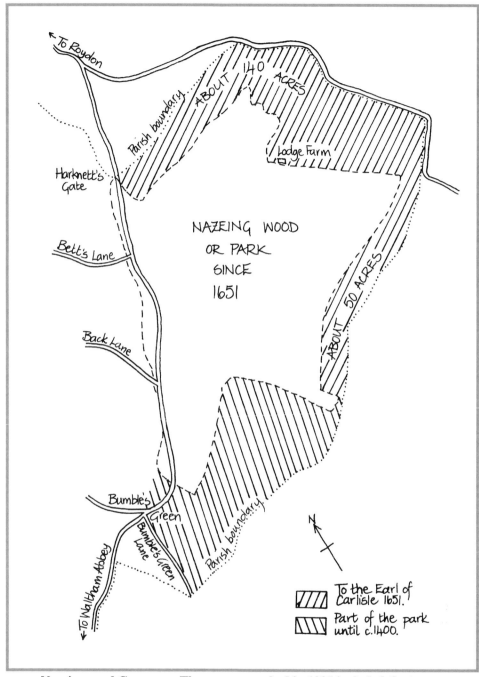

To Roydon

Parish boundary

ABOUT 140 ACRES

Lodge Farm

Harknett's Gate

NAZEING WOOD OR PARK SINCE 1651

Bett's Lane

ABOUT 50 ACRES

Back Lane

Bumbles Green

Bumbles Green Lane

Parish boundary

To Waltham Abbey

N

To the Earl of Carlisle 1651.

Part of the park until c.1400.

Nazeingwood Common. The area emparked in 1225 included the two shaded areas. All the park was overseen from the lodge.

rectangular with rounded corners. Such a shape may be seen at Ongar Great Park, one of only two existing before the Conquest, although its boundary, which was still almost intact in 1950, has been much destroyed since. There was a park lodge, where the parkers did their business, set normally at the highest point and commanding a view of whatever was not hidden by trees. The name 'lodge' has often continued, as at Lodge Farm, which indeed has splendid views over Nazeing Wood or Park. The present area, which has been fixed at about 440 acres since 1651, is not much more than half what was included originally when the shape was roughly rectangular. It included two other large pieces of land. One was towards Bumbles Green, almost up to the parish boundary where it turns at Long Green; this ceased to be part of the park during the fifteenth century, perhaps even a little earlier. The other piece was towards Broadley Common, with a boundary the same as that of the parish. Further evidence of the position of the boundary at the south-western end is the ancient location of the houses with rights on Nazeingwood Common along it, Allmains, Callis, Hawthorn Cottage, and Beverley Cottage. Similarly the Nook and Jacks Hatch Garage are at the north-eastern corner and the positions of Sun Cottage, Collyers, Abbot's Cottage, Kingswood Chase, The Red House, King Harold's Cottage, Ivy Cottages, and Gardner's are along the western boundary. Even when Chapman and André made their map in 1777, the only dwelling within the original confines of the park was the lodge. (See map on previous page.) The area would have held enough deer to enable the abbot to satisfy his frequent royal guests, with some to spare, even without the abutting Harold's Park.

The original position of Nazeing Gate was by the junction of Middle Street and Bumbles Green Lane, which would have been a track beside the park boundary. Allmains, which was perhaps an abbey office, would have been by the entrance. A curiosity about Nazeingwood Common is presented by the approach roads. In the parish and adjacent to it there are only two practically straight stretches constructed before Nazeing New Road in 1909. One is to Harknett's Gate, at one entrance to the park; the other is to Bumbles Green, from perhaps as far as Laundry Lane. It seems likely that these were constructed soon after 1286, when the high fence and new gates were permitted, and that they were intended as impressive approaches. Soon after the construction of the new road from the abbey farmsteads were established along it, spaced out and all on the west side, opposite the Riddens. Those include Pillar Box Cottage, St. Lawrence Farm, Mamelons, and Selways.

The villagers of Nazeing had the right to graze animals in the park, as they did before 1225 when the land was "waste". Even in the thirteenth century the right to graze animals was restricted. The right was in gross, which meant that a total number of animals could be put to graze, whereas the usual system on common land was that a number of animals was permitted to each villager and anyone's shortfall could be made up by the lord of the manor. There seems to have been also a limited right of estover (the taking of wood) but not of lopping, turbary (taking of peat or turf), or pannage (sending pigs to eat the acorns), both of which last were normal on commons. With these peculiarities Nazeing Wood was not strictly a common, although the appellation has been given to it for a long time.

Although there was no mill in 1086, one was rebuilt within the next hundred years and led to a dispute between Walter de Gant, the first abbot of Waltham, and Alan of St. Cross, the prior of the Knights Hospitaller in England. A final concord was reached in November 1190 whereby the Hospitallers would strengthen their weir by the canons' land beside Nazeing mill. This was probably near to where the Crown Inn stands now. They would dam the water between the weir and the mill when they wished to bring water to their mill at Broxbourne. This was done in such a way that there would be no hindrance to shipping and no damage to Nazeing mill or to the canons' land there. They were to pay 4s. per year from Broxbourne mill to the miller at Nazeing. Furthermore the Hospitallers granted and quitclaimed to the canons' farm at Nazeing a fishery at the weir of the old mill at Broxbourne so that they could fish freely at their own weir by Nazeing mill. That did not resolve the matter entirely, for in 1228 a further final concord concerning the fishery was made in the king's court at Westminster. These incidents indicate how important the Lea and its management were to the local economy, as a source of power and food as well as for transport.

The manor courts, held every few weeks in Nazeing, as elsewhere, dealt with transfers of tenure and with related matters. Under feudal law a holding was surrendered to the lord when a tenant died or relinquished his land. Although succession by an heir or heiress became accepted very early, before he or she could take possession an admission fine had to be paid into the lord's court. The courts dealt with petty crimes and torts (civil wrongs) as well, and enforced contracts long before the Common Law took any notice of them. All matters were considered according to the custom of the manor.

The court rolls for Nazeing survive for one year in the thirteenth century and for occasional years in the fifteenth century. The 1270-1 cases, about refusals to perform various obligations, give a picture of a society in which co-operation was normal and disputes were settled fairly amicably, so that contentious matters were dealt with effectively and in a civilised manner.

For example, at the Court held on the Monday after the feast of St. Luke 54 Henry III (20th October 1270)

> Roger Pake asserts against William le Meneter that when he was at the house of Geoffrey Spurling on Sunday before the feast of St. Luke … he insulted the above Roger with abusive words because the aforesaid Roger refused to give a half-penny for a gallon of ale as fixed by the assize and this he did to his damage of 2/-. The aforesaid William being present did not defend himself because he is in mercy [fined] 6d., pledge Walter ate slo.

At the same Court

> Osbert Curteys sues Richard Levenot in that although he was his partner for ploughing his land, he neglected to plough his land as he had promised. Richard replied that he had done nothing contrary to his agreement and thence they put themselves on an inquest on either side. The inquest declares that the said Richard has not kept his agreement as is right and customary, therefore the said Richard is in mercy 6d.; pledges William de Selfe, John Hayward, plaintiff to recover damages 12d. by estimation of six jurors.

At the same Court

> It was presented that the wife of Osbert Curteys has sold ale contrary to the assize, there fore she is in mercy 6d.

At the same Court

> Richard Wrenne gives to the Lord for having licence to give his daughter in marriage 2s.

Court held on Wednesday in Whitweek 55 Henry III (27th May 1271)

> Richard Levenoth was convicted of setting up a stile where one ought not to be made; therefore he is in mercy 12d., pledge John Osegod.

At the same Court

> Dom. G, the prior, leased to William Aylid all the fishery between Wrmelelocke and Brokesburnlocke, to have and to hold as long as he lives, rendering for it yearly at the usual terms 28s., pledges Richard Levenoth, Symon de Selfe.

At the same Court

Roger Pake was convicted of defaming Stephen, the clerk, saying that he ought to associate with robbers, therefore he is in mercy 12d., and he will satisfy the clerk for damages, pledge Walter ate Slo.

The Black Death and its effects

By 1300 the population of England had increased, from about one and three quarter million at the time of the Domesday survey, to about five and a half million. If the population of Nazeing changed in proportion, it would have risen to about 450. It is likely, however. that Nazeing grew somewhat more than average because of the proximity and economic influence of the abbey. In addition to tilling their own and their lord's land, many villeins had earnings on the side from such trades as brewing, carpentry, and holding stalls in a market. In 1235 there had been eighty-four tenants, indicating a population of about 400. There was a marked increase in England's population in the second half of the century. This too indicates the probability of a higher figure at the end of the thirteenth century and indeed suggests that the number of people living in Nazeing was then nearly six hundred. Such a figure is corroborated further if we assume that the population of Nazeing and of England as a whole fell thereafter in proportion to each other. There were sixty-three householders in Nazeing in 1524, signifying a population of almost three hundred when the number of people in England was 2,300,000, less than half what it been in 1300.

We may surmise that in the eleventh century the manor house for the Lower Town had been near either Curtis Farm or the Mansion House. There is no direct evidence for its position or for the position of the manor house of the Upper Town, which was probably near the church. A likely site is that of the Old Vicarage, retained by the canons of Waltham as a residence of the priest when Nazeing Bury became the manor house for both manors. That may have been even before 1200, for it was at Nazeing Bury the manor court was held in the thirteenth century and probably earlier. In 1401 the bery cross (*i.e.* the cross roads) was recorded, indicating that the house was long established. Most of the sites of houses with common rights today were probably in existence by 1300. The villeins' houses seem to have become more spread, with development westwards along Middle Street, on the edges of the park itself , in Hoe Lane on the route between the Upper Town and Nazeing

Bury, at Leonards Green on the Bury Road, near Langridge, and elsewhere. (See map by Chapman and André on front endpaper.)

From this period we have information about many inhabitants who derived their names from dwellings or whose families gave their names to dwellings. These almost certainly include the following: Osebert le Curteys (1270, Curtis Farm), Walter le Neweman (1275, Newmans, recently renamed Felsteads), Walter Campe (1277, Camps), John le Proust de Nasingg (1285, Profits Hill Cottages, Little Profits), Alexander Kydiere (1308, Nether Kidders); then William de Langrich (Langridge), William de Maresco/Marisco (Marshgate Farm), John Shadewater (Shadwalkers), and John and Richard atte Pyrie/Pirie (Perry Hill Farm), all in 1327; and later, Henry Coliere (1400, Collyers), William Gardiner (1400, Gardner's, now Common View), William Mapel (1400, Maplecroft), John Payne (1400, Paynes Farm), John Snowe (1400, Snowes, very recently renamed Laun House), Thomas Warle (1400, Warleys, very recently renamed Feltre), Richard White (1400, White's Wood Cottage), John Laurence (1403, Lawrence, later Saint Lawrence, Farm), John Maryon (1416 Marions, later Mamelons, very recently renamed Valley View), John Motte (1475, Motts, since earlier this century Walnut Tree Cottages), and Robert Wheler (1475, Wheelers). All the houses mentioned have rights on Nazeing Wood or Park.

The area of land under cultivation at the beginning of the fourteenth century was similar to that six hundred years later but, with the mediaeval system of agriculture, what was produced could sustain no more than the existing population. It was not until the Agricultural Revolution started in the early eighteenth century that the number of people in England exceeded five and a half million. Meanwhile a lower birth rate, the effect of which was accentuated by devastating famine and disease in the early fourteenth century, especially the Great Famine of 1316 to 1317, caused a decline in the number of inhabitants. Then came the shattering blow of the Black Death. If Nazeing was similar to Codicote, which is not far away, almost half the population died in the winter and spring of 1348-9. It has been suggested that the barrow on Garlands, a field behind Mansion House Farm, is where the victims of the plague were buried. Later outbreaks in 1361, 1369, 1371, and 1375 would have taken a further toll. No event ever had a more cataclysmic effect on the lives of the people of Nazeing.

A century at least before 1350 there had been a considerable movement of population. People went from one village to another or sought their fortune in towns. A John of Nazeing went to London, became a brewer, and, when he died in 1356, left considerable property to St. Mary-at-Hill in Billingsgate, close to which church was Abbot Walter's stone house, the London headquarters of canons of Waltham from before 1200 until the Dissolution. Another John of Nazeing became a girdler in London later in the century.

Such movements caused a market in smallholdings to develop. A trend had been established already for strips in open fields to be exchanged to create blocks which could then be enclosed as small private fields. This became more frequent so that many holdings were fairly compact. Women were often the absolute owners, so that marrying widows or daughter heiresses was a way in which single men could acquire land. The famines and then, to an even greater degree, the Black Death, caused a much greater movement of people and increased the rate at which land changed hands. So, towards 1400, as the fitter or more entrepreneurial built up their holdings, there began to develop what became the norm, in Nazeing as elsewhere, small farms employing labourers. Enclosures took place gradually. A court roll of 1456 mentions small parcels of land in Northfield, Highfield, and Upper Town ("Obertown") which were presumably open fields. Pressfield, a large open field in the north of the parish, was named in 1400, though it had been divided and enclosed by 1767. As the houses were spread widely by 1400 most, perhaps almost all, had their own enclosed fields adjacent. The fields owned in 1624 as part of Curtis Farm are ascertained from its deeds but, from the number of species of tree in the hedges, it seems that the boundaries had been established a century or more earlier. The boundaries of Goodalls and other properties seem to be of similar age. The normal holding was becoming no longer strips in open fields but a group or two of small enclosed fields, together with rights in the meads and in Nazeing Wood.

The famines and the plague had dealt an irreparable blow to the community spirit. Rising discontent during the 1370s culminated in the Peasants' Revolt of 1381, which started in Brentwood and almost at once spread to the whole of Essex. Villeins became much less willing to support one another and by the early fifteenth century tenants resorted to violence frequently, to right wrongs and to solve feuds. In 1411 "Nicholas Webbe of Nasing, on the feast of St. Bartholomew, armed with hauberks, plates, palettes, sticks, glaives, bows, arrows, swords, and darts, leagued with 200 others to kill John Walden, Sheriff of Essex, and broke into the Close of the Abbot of Waltham, also releasing prisoners in the hand of the Sheriff at the same time." On 9th November, 1415, Henry V issued a Commission to John Petrie, Sergeant at Arms, to arrest John Grove, John Cademan, and Robert Brewer, all Nazeing farmers, and to bring them with all possible speed before the King. Whether the commission was carried out is not recorded but Brewer fell foul of the law again. On 24th November, 1423, it was reported to the Crown Law Officers that certain tenants, farmers of Nazeing, had met together and bound themselves to one another by oath to resist the Sheriff, Lewis John, and his assistants and that they absolutely refused to perform any of their services as tenants of the Abbot of Waltham. On 31st December the sheriff summoned to Westminster, among others, Robert Brewer and Nicholas Symond, both farmers, and William Carter, a fletcher, all of Nazeing, "for having arranged themselves in manner of war against the sheriff, lain in wait for him at Waltham Abbey with the intention to slay him, and having beset him in a certain house there and so threatened him with death and mutilation, and abused him, that for a long time he could not execute a certain writ of the King directed to him as sheriff."

Another indication of lack of commitment to the village was that in 1442 the vicar had allowed the Vicarage to fall to the ground. Perhaps this was the nadir of the village's fortune. There is a tradition that the mediaeval Vicarage was where the Upper Town Post Office stands today, though it seems improbable that the Vicarage was so far from the church. Certainly the Old Post Office would have been built soon after 1440; it is the only house in Nazeing hardly altered since that time. Before it became the post office it was called Moat Farm from the moat round it, parts of which still exist. The Old Vicarage too is older than the outside suggests.

We may assume anyway that the Vicarage was rebuilt soon after 1442, before extensive improvements were made to All Saints' Church. The north aisle and the present chancel were added and the nave was reroofed. Then, towards the end of the fifteenth century, the tower was built, in brick in a style adopted widely in Essex between 1490 and 1530. The bricks seem to have been made at the same brickfield as those used in the construction of the gatehouse at Nether Hall and to have been laid in a similar style. The gatehouse was built in the late fifteenth century, so the suggestion on a board in the church that the tower is more recent does not stand up to scrutiny. From the south All Saints' looked then much as it does today, as the only major changes to the exterior have been the building of the vestry in 1891 and the Pilgrim Room in 1999, and the removal of the spire in 1899. (See pictures on jacket and page 125.)

Two of Nazeing's oldest properties from photographs of around 1910. Both are jettied hall-houses dating from 1500 or earlier. Above is the Old Post Office from a postcard. Below is Greenleaves, with David Pegrum and his wife.

The gradual return of prosperity

By the second half of the fifteenth century, and probably considerably earlier, the abbot and canons of Waltham had given up managing their manor of Nazeing through a steward and had let it to tenant farmers. An indenture of 1502, setting out the terms of a lease of Nazeing Bury by the Abbot of Waltham to John Nankotton, a merchant of London, notes that the previous tenant had been George Congreve, who may well have held the manor for some years. Nankotton, like his predecessors presumably, was subject to terms similar to those of a modern farming lease and had to deal with the abbey's cellarer.

Langridge, in the south-west corner of the parish, had become a free tenement of the abbey. It had probably belonged to the Fitz Auchers of Copped Hall, who were Foresters from the twelfth to the fourteenth centuries. William Langridge, who owned the manor subsequently, belonged to a family prominent in the area in the fourteenth century. From him the manor passed in time to Richard Waldern who died in 1488 leaving it to his three daughters, the husband of one of whom was described as a fishmonger, that of another as a gentleman. The holdings of Nazeing Bury and of Langridge indicate how already those who made a good living by trade obtained interests in land, though they may have treated their holdings just as investments and never have lived in the village.

During the final years of the abbey at Waltham the area seems to have been what estate agents call "desirable". Matilda Parr, the mother of Katherine, leased the rights to timber and wood in Nazeing Wood from the abbot in 1527. In the sixteenth century the term 'woodland' did not mean a thick wood; it described an area from which wood could be obtained and could even include hedgerows with trees. Wood was used for fencing, wattlework, and so on but mostly for burning; timber was the large trees used for building. There is no evidence for the suggestion that Matilda Parr (or her daughter, Katharine) ever lived in Nazeing, so presumably she thought it worthwhile to have her wood carted a considerable distance. Thomas Cromwell, Lord Privy Seal and Vicar-General, is reported to have been the tenant of Nazeing Bury in 1533 and, by somewhat dubious means, of Langridge in 1534. Two of Henry VIII's chancellors had strong associations with neighbouring parishes: Cardinal Wolsey owned Cheshunt Great House; Sir Thomas More married Jane Colte of Nether Hall. Further, Sir Anthony Denny was the courtier who was so close to the king that he had the task of telling him that he was dying. Therefore he must have had a good choice of land seized from the monasteries. He picked Waltham itself, and with it the manor of Nazeing. That the population had held up in 1524, compared with England generally since 1300, confirms the agricultural prosperity brought about in part by the Abbey's good management. This, and their proximity to London, made Nazeing and district desirable.

Another reason why Henry VIII's chancellors were attracted to the area may have been the king's own association. He had an affection for Waltham Abbey and possibly he had a direct association with Nazeing, as a hunting stand was put up in his time at Greenmead, the land at the Jack's Hatch end of Nazeingwood Common. This stand was at a point with a good view over the immediate terrain, where a launde, or open space, was cleared so that the deer could be seen more easily. The stand was improved in 1542. Greenmead was excluded specifically from the area leased to Matilda Parr, presumably because the abbot did not want her men interfering with the undergrowth and trees left to funnel the deer in front of the stand.

Sir Anthony Denny was a friend and courtier of King Henry VIII. After the dissolution of the monasteries he was granted the lands of Waltham Abbey, including Nazeing. Painted by Holbein in 1549.

Waltham, the richest abbey in Essex and the most important Austin house in England, was the last monastery in England to be dissolved, on 23rd March 1540. Some of the dependants who were pensioned off lived in Nazeing already or came to live there. Among them were John Peycock, Robert and Richard Curteyss, and William Shelley, some of whose descendants sailed for the New World a century later. In the sale of abbey furnishings, many of which were bought by Anthony Denny, those taken from Nazeing church included "a tunicle of white bawdekyn with coper gold (for the King's use), two coopes of grene sylke wroughte with byrdes and floures (sold for 13s.0d), and two coopes of redd counterfett sylver (sold for 10s.0d)". With the items described went almost certainly the church's silver. The advowson was appropriated by the King and, as Nazeing was not a rich living, passed on to the Lord Chancellor. The rectory, which carried the right to receive the tithes, stayed with the manor.

In 1541 the Crown granted to Denny a thirty-one year lease of much of the land formerly owned by Waltham Abbey. This included "the

The seal and signatures of the Abbot and Canons to the surrender of Waltham Abbey.

manor of Nasynge *alias* Nasingbury, a close called Quenemead and all lands in Nasing lately in the hands of Matilda Parr, rectory of Nasynge and tithes, lately devised to Tho. Cromwell Kt. late of Essex." In 1544 Sir Ralph Sadler, who had found fortune as an assistant of Cromwell, paid £1837.1s.8d to the King for the reversion of the manor of Nazeing and of the lands in the estate of the late Dame Matilda Parr, as well as other property in Gloucester and London. In the following year, however, Denny's lease was extended for a further twenty-five years, in return for a payment into the Augmentation Fund which the king had established. Denny, who had been knighted in 1544, died five years later. His widow obtained outright ownership of the manors of Waltham and Nazeing just before the death of Edward VI, in 1553.

Thus, after a decade or so of uncertainty, the manor of Nazeing, for so long in the hands of Waltham, was owned once more by a lay individual. The Denny family lived in Waltham Abbey, so that little changed in Nazeing, with Nazeing Bury occupied by a tenant, as before, and Langridge still under separate ownership and having a tenant. Much of the land in the village, perhaps almost all except the meads by the Lea and Stoneshott Common, had been enclosed and was held by copyhold tenure. Apart from the roads shown on Chapman and André's map, in the mid sixteenth century there were also other lanes, such as Church Lane (described on page 28) and Madlands Lane which ran from Middle Street, beside Darmers, over Walker's Hill, and on to the meadows by the brook. The routes of such lanes are still rights of way, or were so until very recently. Nazeing Wood or Park was wooded but not densely so; the Dennys continued to keep fallow deer in it for some years after gaining possession. The rightholders continued to run their animals with the deer and to retain their other rights. Matilda Parr's lease must have conflicted with their right of estover, presaging bitter disputes to come. Much of the Upper Town Post Office and small parts of the present Ninnings, Greenleaves, and Nazeing Bury had been built in about 1500 but there was only one building instantly recognisable today, having been little altered since then - All Saints' Church. Thus Nazeing appeared in the final years of the reign of Henry VIII.

A document has survived in the King's own hand expressing his intention to endow a number of bishoprics. At the head of the list is Waltham, designated as the cathedral city of Essex. With the King's death, early in 1547, the plan lapsed. Had he survived longer, the following chapters might have been a little different.

Nazeing Bury, part of which dates from about 1500, from a photograph in about 1900. Below is a recent photograph of Lodge Farm which has a commanding view over Nazeingwood Common.

Mr J Wilkinson   1 copy/copies   Refund £ 5
Ashmead

"Five Miles from Everywhere"
The Story of Nazeing from Early Times to 1914

Thank you for your order, in advance of publication, for this
first volume of the history of our village.

We are sorry that it is later than originally promised, but
the good news is that the printing costs have turned out
to be less than expected.

As the price is now £10 instead of £15 your refund is enclosed.

Further copies of this volume are available from the following
members of the Nazeing History Workshop -

Doug Ball	01992 463634
Colin Dauris	01992 893114
Valerie Day	01992 893154
John Garbutt	01992 893906
Paddy Hutchings	01992 892001
Russell Martin	01992 892169
David Pracy	01992 893264

and we will advise you when Volume 2 is ready.

CHAPTER 3

"A FAIR FORTUNE IN LAND"

Turbulent times, 1547 to 1660

The period from the Reformation to the Restoration was one of political, social, economic and religious upheaval in England. The national population doubled, and economic and social problems multiplied. In the 1590s a succession of disastrous harvests led to the first serious famine in almost 300 years, and in the 1640s civil war broke out for the first time since 1485. Nazeing shared fully in the national unrest, so this was probably the most turbulent time in its history.

The new lords of the manor

After the death of Henry VIII, the young King Edward VI leased the Waltham Abbey estates to Sir Anthony Denny, who died in 1549. In 1553 Edward granted them outright to Denny's widow Joan, but later the same year she and the king both died. Nazeing passed to Henry, son of Anthony and Joan, who, as soon as he came of age, went on a substantial spending spree. He paid for it by leasing out some 20,000 acres, and for twenty days in 1570 pawned the whole estate. By 1576 however, he and his elder son Robert had died and Henry's younger son, seven-year-old Edward, became lord of the manor. At first the estates were managed by his uncle, who was also something of a spendthrift.

Knighted in 1589, Sir Edward Denny embarked on a political and administrative career and became an M.P., first for Liskeard in Cornwall and then, in 1604, for Essex. He was appointed Commissioner of Sewers for the Lea, a post which gave him responsibility for flood relief measures and for arbitration in disputes between bargemen and millers. A bridge at Dobbs Weir was little used because of high tolls, and so the bridge at Broxbourne mill was one of the most important crossings from Hertfordshire into Essex. When therefore in 1621 it was "in great decay and very dangerous", the Essex Quarter Sessions ordered Denny and the miller to mend it.

Perhaps partly to further his political career, in 1590 Denny married Mary, daughter of Queen Elizabeth's powerful minister Lord Burghley, who lived over the Lea at Theobalds. Sir Edward and Lady Mary soon had a daughter, Honora, but they had no more children. When in 1603

King James I came south to claim his new kingdom, Denny as High Sheriff of Hertfordshire greeted him at Royston and gave him a splendid horse. Among the entourage of Scottish nobles accompanying the king was his friend James Hay, who soon began to seek the hand of the most eligible heiress in England, Honora Denny. Hay's spendthrift reputation had gone before him so father and daughter were less than enthusiastic about the prospect of yet another wastrel in the family, but King James encouraged this alliance between his English and Scottish aristocracy, and in 1607 James Hay and Honora Denny were married.

Edward was created Lord Denny of Waltham and, as part of the marriage settlement, bestowed upon his daughter and son-in-law what the Earl of Clarendon in his *History of the Rebellion* described as "a fair fortune in land", including Nazeing. Despite Honora's misgivings, she and James soon had two children but in 1613 she was attacked by a thief while driving in her coach down Ludgate Hill and died of a miscarriage brought on by the shock. Hay later married Lucy Percy, daughter of the Earl of Northumberland. He had been fined and imprisoned for his indirect involvement in the Gunpowder Plot and Hay used his influence with the King to negotiate his father-in-law's release. In 1622 King James created Hay Earl of Carlisle, named from Carlisle Island, now Barbados, which Hay owned. Lucy Carlisle became a confidante of Henrietta, queen of

James Hay, 1st Earl of Carlisle, was lord of the manor of Nazeing and "surely a man of the greatest expense in his own person of any in the age he lived". Portrait after Van Dyck.

48

Charles I, who succeeded James I in 1625. Carlisle remained in royal favour and in 1629 King Charles intervened illegally on his side in a dispute over West Indian trading rights. Both James and Charles sent him on a variety of diplomatic missions, so he had little involvement with Nazeing; the estates continued to be managed in practice by Lord Denny, who in 1626 was created Earl of Norwich by Charles.

Though none of the Dennys ever lived in Nazeing, they had homes at Waltham Abbey and there was always a strong gentry presence nearby. Initially they were at Dallance, about a mile south of Harold's Park; then Edward built the Abbey House out of stone from the ruined abbey. They had relatives by marriage living at Harold's Park, first Sir Edward Greville, who had married Henry Denny's widow, and later Greville's son-in-law, Sir Francis Swift, who also owned much of Roydon. Swift was the grandson of Queen Elizabeth's auditor, the "beloved friend" of Lord Denny, and, when Denny died in 1637, executor of his will.

James Hay had died the previous year. Clarendon's vivid account of his life shows that Denny's worries about his son-in-law's extravagance had been fully justified.

He was surely a man of the greatest expense in his own person of any in the age he lived, and introduced more of that expense in the excess of clothes and diet than any other man ... and had no other consideration of land than for the support of his lustre; and whilst he could do that he cared not

James Hay, 2nd Earl of Carlisle, was declared by Parliament a delinquent. His largely unsuccessful attempt to recover his fortunes resulted in the "singular case" of Nazeing Wood or Park.

49

for money, having no bowels in the point of running in debt or borrowing all he could ... He left behind him a reputation of a very fine gentleman and a most accomplished courtier, and after having spent, in a very jovial life, above £400,000, which upon a strict computation he received from the crown, he left not a house or acre of land to be remembered ...

This damning indictment was accurate, although its complete fulfilment took half a century. The estates passed to James's son, the 2nd Earl of Carlisle, also James. He married Margaret Russell, daughter of the 4th Earl of Bedford, but they had no children. When he died in 1660, the family's dynastic and financial affairs fell into a state of chaos, which has been expertly disentangled by Dr. John Gervis, whose book can be consulted for further detail. Carlisle's heir was the nephew of Lord Denny, the noted Royalist general Lord George Goring, who had, in 1633, borrowed £20,000 from a Merchant Taylor named Isaac Jones.

Eventually Goring's four married daughters inherited not only the estates but also the debts accumulated by the Carlisles and Gorings over the previous half century. So, during the 1680s, they sold the Nazeing properties to Isaac's great grandson, Samuel Wake Jones, who became the new lord of the manor.

The villagers

Between 1520 and 1640 the population of England roughly doubled and Nazeing followed the national trend. In 1524 Henry VIII and his chief minister Cardinal Wolsey needed money for the war against France and raised a tax called the Lay Subsidy, which was paid by 63 Nazeing men. The next comparable tax for which records survive was the Hearth Tax, instituted after the Restoration; in 1671 119 householders were assessed, almost twice as many. A comparison of the two lists shows that the social structure changed little and that the villagers can be divided into four broad groups.

At the top of the pyramid were gentlemen who held property in Nazeing and possibly lived in the village, but had more extensive social and economic contacts than the other groups. In 1524 the wealthiest man by far was "John Gylys Gent", a member of Wolsey's staff; his goods were assessed at £50, on which he paid 50s, while on goods "elsewhere in the household of the Lord Cardinal" he paid a further 66s. In 1602 George Dyer was buried in the chancel of Nazeing church and bequeathed 20s to the poor of the village; in addition he left £5 to the

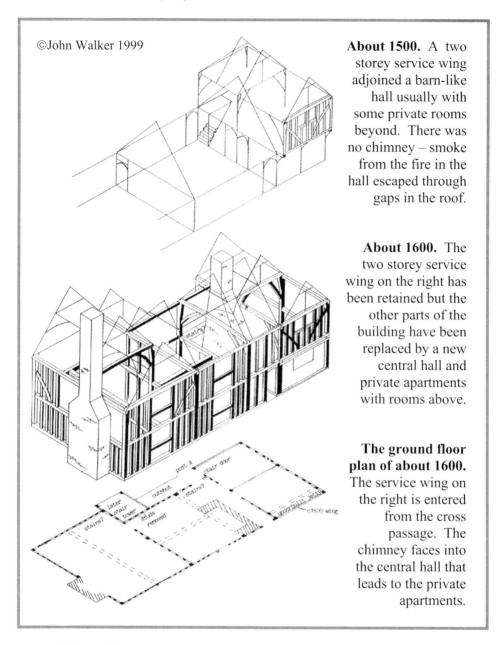

©John Walker 1999

About 1500. A two storey service wing adjoined a barn-like hall usually with some private rooms beyond. There was no chimney – smoke from the fire in the hall escaped through gaps in the roof.

About 1600. The two storey service wing on the right has been retained but the other parts of the building have been replaced by a new central hall and private apartments with rooms above.

The ground floor plan of about 1600. The service wing on the right is entered from the cross passage. The chimney faces into the central hall that leads to the private apartments.

The development of Darmers, a typical yeoman farmer's hall-house.

poor of Albury in Hertfordshire and had connections with Hunsdon in Hertfordshire and Roydon, Harlow, and Great Dunmow in Essex. In the 1630s William King built up a substantial estate in Nazeing and became foreman of the jury, and yet was described as "gent of Hodson

[Hoddesdon]"; his son, William King junior, bought three properties in Nazeing but was a "citizen and haberdasher of London" who played no recorded part in its affairs.

Around one-third of Nazeing household heads were prosperous yeomen who formed the resident elite. Most farmed thirty to fifty acres and employed several labourers. They occupied substantial farmhouses such as Belchers and Camps, many of which were rebuilt in the period from 1570 to 1640, a great age of building and the heyday of the yeoman in England. The combination of poor harvests and increased population caused severe inflation and food prices rose faster than wages. When there was a good harvest the yeomen stored their surplus produce, which they could then sell at a large profit in a bad year when prices were high. This policy was pursued rather too zealously by a Nazeing yeoman named Thomas Burn, who in 1611 bought up fifty quarters of wheat, malt, and barley worth £44 with the intention of reselling them at a profit. Such speculation with other farmers' produce was illegal and so one, Stephen Chandler laid information against him in the hope of being awarded half of the money. Burn appeared in court to answer the accusation but the outcome is not recorded. The inflation gradually widened the gap between haves and have-nots, so that by 1671 five Nazeing yeomen were prosperous enough to be ranked with the minor gentry.

Below the yeomen were the husbandmen and craftsmen, probably living in rather smaller houses such as Smalldrinks and Goodalls. Theirs was a tough life, and they had to eke out a living by growing and tending a range of crops and livestock in order to balance the inevitable failures from disease and pests. They employed the time-honoured method of spreading manure from the back of a cart and then ploughing it in but their yields and even those of the wealthier farmers were tiny compared with yields today. Husbandmen were normally self-sufficient; in a bad year, however, they could suffer severe hardship and sometimes they turned to crime. They usually farmed only ten to fifteen acres, so they could seldom afford to employ labour outside their immediate families and often supplemented their income with small-scale activities such as alehouse-keeping or charcoal-burning. Conversely, craftsmen, whose occupations recorded in this period include a bricklayer, a carpenter, a clothmaker, a fishmonger, a sawyer, a shoemaker, a silk-weaver, a tailor, and a turner, had smallholdings on which they grew much of their own food. How an individual was described was therefore often a matter of personal choice and self-perception.

At the bottom of the social scale were labourers and the poor, who were almost entirely dependent for their existence on the better off. Their original cottages were too flimsy to have survived, although some of the present-day common right houses such as the Red House are later, more substantial replacements. They were hardest hit by the inflation: their real wages, which were never high, dropped by 25 per cent between 1583 and 1602, and did not recover until the eighteenth century. The harsh Poor Law introduced in 1597 differentiated between deserving poor, who received a minimum of charity, and the undeserving, who were forced to work. Parishes became responsible for their own poor, so that those who could not prove a "settlement" were moved back to their parish of origin. Nazeing parish register entries for "a wandering woman, buried September 1599" and "a wandering boy, buried Jan.8th, 1601" probably record early casualties of this policy. Many of the more prosperous classes made provision for the poor in their wills, craftsmen and husbandmen perhaps only 12d but yeomen anything up to £10.

Fortunately the parish registers for Nazeing survive from 1559, recording baptisms, marriages, and burials at All Saints'. There was at all levels of society considerable family continuity, with names such as Algar, Camp, Pegrum, Shelley, and Wilkinson recurring. These names were common throughout west Essex and there were strong links of kinship as families moved around the area, though it is not always clear how closely people with the same surname were related or how long particular families remained settled in Nazeing. Certainly an established name was no guarantee of social position: Robert Holmes, though related to a Sir William Holmes, was a simple husbandman with little in the way of goods or land, while in 1662 John Camp was living at Snowes, a seven-hearth house, whereas five other Camps were occupying humble cottages.

Still according to the customs of the manor

Manorial courts continued much as they had through mediaeval times, although their importance gradually declined as parishes were given new responsibilities such as the Poor Law. Very few official manorial records for Nazeing survive from before 1669 but there is a splendid collection of draft notes for the courts of 1637-8. They were written in English by William Hone, the steward of Waltham Abbey and Nazeing, and give homely details which may not have found their way

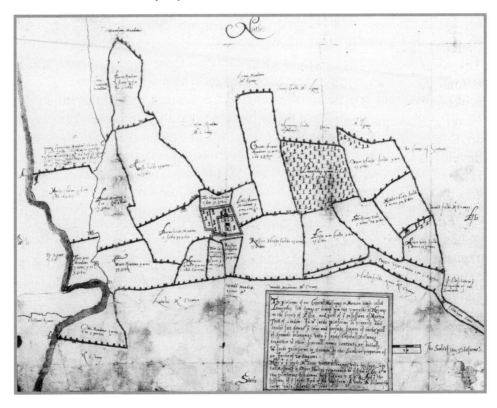

A map "of one Capytall Messuage or Mancon howse called Langrydge ... ye possessions of Martyn Trott ..." drawn in about 1600.

into the more formal Latin record that is now lost. These papers provide a vivid portrait of Nazeing life at that time.

In 1637 the Earls of Carlisle and Norwich (James Hay and Edward Denny) had died recently, so the jury produced for the new lord of the manor (the 2nd Earl of Carlisle) a custumal. In this they claimed their rights, many dating back "time out of mind", with a selection of excerpts from the manorial records of the previous 25 years. This was of crucial importance because the new lord and the tenants would both have been keen to assert their customary rights. Although the document is a record of the jury's concerns and omits issues benefiting the Earl, thus not providing the whole picture, it is still an invaluable insight into the period.

The custumal includes a list of 79 "Coppieholders and freeholders belonging to this mannor of Nazing", headed by ten "gents" and three "clerkes". At the top of the list is Martin Trott, whose family owned Langridge for over a century; there are other familiar names such as John Tey, who probably held the farm which still bears his name. "Edward Palmer Esq." was the examining magistrate when, in 1641, four men broke down the altar-rails at Latton Church. Later George Palmer of Nazeing Park claimed descent from him. George was certainly related to an Edward Palmer who in 1673 bought the property which was later developed into Nazeing Park, although Edward does not appear on Hearth Tax returns for the intervening period and it is unclear whether he was the same man.

Perhaps the most remarkable name on the steward's list is that of "Cheshunt men freeholders". When in 1622 James I and Lord Burghley exchanged their palaces of Hatfield House and Theobalds, the king extended the grounds of the latter by acquiring part of the neighbouring common; this was a high-handed action which outraged the freeholders of Cheshunt. Although unable to recover their common land, they succeeded in winning £500 compensation, of which they spent £180 on building almshouses in Turners Hill for ten aged widows. The freeholders provided for the continuing support of the poor by investing the remaining £320 in buying the sixteen acres now known as Curtis Farm, which remained the property of Cheshunt parish until the twentieth century. One of the Trustees was Sir Thomas Dacres who, like Sir Francis Swift, was an executor of Edward Denny's will.

In these turbulent times, proper husbanding and regulation of scarce resources could literally be a matter of life and death, so that the jury's two main concerns were exercise of common rights and unauthorised building of new homes. A custom had evolved attaching one right on Nazeingwood Common to each of 98 older houses, regardless of size. This alleviated the plight of those poorer people entitled to rights but others, in desperation, often encroached on the common. A provision that "none shall common in Nasinge Wood [unless] he dwell in an ancient ten[emen]t" was put forward three times in as many years, showing that in conservation of village resources the jury had common sense in both senses of the phrase. In 1614 "the jury presented and pained that none who dwell in new erected tents shall comon in Nasinge Wood", and the next year four men were each amerced 40s for doing so. In 1624 John Holly and Robert Goudge were presented "for buyldinge of two cottages", while the following year the jury presented "new erected tents" by Holly, Goudge and nine others. In 1629 the jury pained that "there shall not be ij [2] Commoners for one tent in Nasinge", and in 1637 that

> noe mann in Nasinge wch holdeth any land out of the Towne shall not [sic] at any tyme bring their Cattell out of that lande to Common in any our commons in Nasynge on payne to forfeit for every tyme so taken x s [10s].

A similar forfeit of five shillings was to be paid for taking in "anye Cattell for other mens to put upon any of our commons". Such prohibitions were often an attempt to exclude outsiders from valuable resources and references to "our commons" show a strong sense of community. Most of those presented had well-established Nazeing surnames and had strongly felt obligations to their neighbours, to many of whom they were related.

The steward's papers also contain a record of "Pains and orders made by the Homage at his Ma<u>ties</u> Leet the Lordes Court Baron ther holden the last day of Maye 1637", a detailed account of the first court held for the new lord of the manor. It was concerned mostly with property transactions and minor agricultural misdemeanours.

Property continued to be either freehold or copyhold. The word freehold had a similar meaning to that of today and freeholders could buy and sell property as they wished. Copyhold land also was privately owned but transactions in it were recorded in the court records and a copy was given to each new tenant. Their land was described as copyhold because they held a copy. They were also known as customary tenants because they held their land from the lord of the manor and became tenants at a court "according to the customs of the Manor". The term "landlord" was derived from the relationship between the lord of the manor and his customary tenants, who swore an oath of allegiance to him and in return received protection from the court which established local laws according to the customs of the manor. Although there was no clear cut distinction, copyholders tended to be of lower status than freeholders. Freehold transactions and details about sub-tenants, who were usually landless labourers, were rarely noted in the manorial records, which therefore tell us most about those in the middle ranks of village society.

Customary tenants had to follow a procedure of surrender and admission. The transaction took place in the manorial court, where each of the participants grasped a symbolic stick called the rod held out by the lord or his representative and the purchaser paid an entry fee called a fine. These fines were levied even where land was transferred within a family following the death of the previous owner, and sometimes they were so substantial that the heir had either to sell the land or to borrow money using it as security. For this reason, it was not uncommon for land and the cost of the fine to be bequeathed together in wills. An example of this is the 1621 will of a yeoman-farmer named Benet Eliot where, following the distribution of his property, his executors were to "pay all such fine or fines as shall be due to the Lord or Lords for theire sayde lands when they shall be thereunto admitted ..."

The steward's papers contain summaries of about twenty surrenders "into the hande of the lorde of the manor of Nazinge accordinge to the rodde by the custome of the said manor". In practice the work was normally done by the meticulous William Hone. Next to each transaction he notes the entry fine, his own fee (a standard 5s.) and a note of the rent. Entry fines were substantial, anything from £10 to £75, but rents were usually only four or five shillings per annum. One of the steward's most important tasks was to search the records for previous transactions. At the end of Hone's notes for the August 1638 court is a very human touch: he has written himself a reminder to "see for a former surr[ender], made by Margarett Rennols entered in my tyme... Make a Copy of Widow Tysones adm 5s for Jo. Reade..." Surrenders were made to various pairs of jurymen who perhaps found this task rather a chore. John Shelley was often chosen, which may be why Hone noted, in a wonderful mixture of English and dog Latin, that he "refuse to be of the jury - ergo in mias" [therefore was placed at the mercy of the lord].

The individual transactions show how properties (some of them identifiable today) were transferred within families or sold. Thomas Huchins was a juror who in 1637 was himself presented for not scouring a ditch. The following year he was suddenly taken ill and lying "in extreme". As he had not made a will, he dictated his wishes to two other jurors, leaving his property (Cotlands, now Cutlands) to his wife and after her death to his son John. The inheritance, however, was somewhat double-edged, for within two years of her death John had to pay £10 to his brother Thomas and within four years another £10 was to go to a second brother, William. Furthermore

> ...for fault of payment of this twentie pounds they or eyther of them should enter upon the said messuage and premises and the same hold till he or they pay themselves out of it...

To aggravate the apparent injustice, William was to receive a comparably sized farm (Newmans, now Felsteads) with no similar strings attached.

57

Robert Keyes was a substantial landowner whose family had been in Nazeing since at least 1524; they gave their name to Keysers Estate. Robert surrendered his property on 17th May 1638 and Hone recorded his will, dated five days earlier. Robert had three sons. Robert junior was a considerable owner in his own right and is not mentioned in the will. The bulk of the property, including Robert's own house, went to Samuel. Nathaniel had died before his father but had had a son John to whom Robert left "a tent called Ruxbourer" (almost certainly Sturtsbury Farm) and accompanying lands, for which the entry fee was an apparently exorbitant £75. Robert died soon after and was buried at All Saints' on 21st July 1638, aged about 80. In the same year a stone bearing the names of Robert Keyse (whether senior or junior is unclear) and William Campe was placed on the west wall of the church, probably because they were churchwardens when major repairs were done.

Margaret Rennols, for whom Hone reminded himself to check a previous surrender, was a prosperous widow who owned a substantial property called Makerells. It comprised a late medieval dwelling on or near the site of the present Mulberries, together with some eighteen acres. She wanted to divide it between her grand-daughters, Joan Adams and Mary Curtis, who were to share not only the land but also the house, which Hone therefore described in some detail. Mary was to have

> the Hall and all the West End of the said Messuage and the great Barne with the west part of the foreyard from the greate post of the hall to the great gate, and the west Parte of the Backyard from the middle post betweene the two windowes to the end of the pales together allso with the close adioining to the Backside of the said messuage conteyning eight Akers...

Joan had the remaining ten acres and the east end of the house.

In this period the rate at which the ownership of land passed out of the village accelerated. John Reade the younger, a Nazeing carpenter, sold Nether Kidders to Margaret Waylett, wife of a Harlow yeoman. Robert Keyes junior sold one piece of land in Nazeing Mead to Nicholas Brewett of "Waltham Hollicross" and another to William King of Hoddesdon. King also bought Coldhams Croft, the field immediately north of Colemans Lane (formerly Coldhams Lane), from Margaret Rennols and her family. This trend was to prove very significant in the following 150 years.

Minor agricultural misdemeanours were dealt with by the thirteen-man jury, whose names are recorded; it is easy to imagine these senior farmers and craftsmen walking the fields to note the transgressions.

Often the jury did not fine the culprit immediately but imposed a "pain" if he did not mend his ways. George Shelley and John Waylett of Roydon Hamlet were each presented for leaving marl to lie in the highway: Shelley was pained 20s "if he doe not carrye the same betwene this and 2 of July next" whereas Waylett was pained 40s but given till 29th September to remove it. Perhaps his pile was bigger.

Crime and punishment

The manorial courts dealt with minor problems, but more serious matters were tried at county assizes and quarter sessions, presided over by Justices of the Peace who had the unimpeded right to regulate in minutest detail the lives of their social subordinates. Essex records are among the best preserved in the country and give a good insight into the less respectable side of Nazeing life.

Quarter sessions dealt with administrative as well as criminal matters, and some offences which might today be regarded as civil misdemeanours were seen as serious enough to go before the higher courts. In 1617 John Campe was indicted for enclosing and obstructing "with bushes and a wood a common footway leading from a messuage called Ninnetts [Ninnings] to Nazeing church where it crosses his messuage called Stonnycroft". In 1627 George Curtis "stayed" a watercourse across the highway from Nazeing to Waltham Abbey, and his "likewise annoying the same place by laying his dung [was] very dangerous". By "throwing out his dung" Nicholas Goodgame was in 1664 a great "predgeise to his neighbours".

Matters of morality also could come before the courts when they resulted in a charge upon the parish. In 1611 Robert Greygoose, labourer, was accused of fornication with Mary Mostinge " who is now brought abedd and delivered of a child". In 1624 Elizabeth Munster, spinster of Nazeing, was delivered in Lambourne of a bastard child and confessed the father to be John Peach of Lambourne, who was served with a bastardy order and ordered to pay.

Repeated presentments of the same individuals for keeping disorderly alehouses without licence suggest a lack of sanctions to enforce the law. John Cooke was presented twice in 1612; after his death his widow carried on the family tradition, being admonished three times in five years. During the 1640s a husbandmen named Robert Sawell was presented at Chelmsford six times for the same misdemeanour.

Evidently he learnt from the experience, though not perhaps in the way intended by the bench: he moved to the county town, where he became an innholder and was presented for helping a customer "drink and tipple on the Sabbath Day".

One of the most frequent crimes was forcible entry to private parks for poaching. In 1586 various malefactors broke into Nazeing Wood, then held by Edward Greville Esq., to hunt roe deer. In 1589 Geoffrey Pond of Epping, Robert Campe of Nazeing, and Richard Grove of "Little Pingdon [Parndon]" were indicted for poaching, having entered Nazeing Wood with four greyhounds and hunted and killed seven does. In 1595 another gang assaulted two of Greville's servants and took away two bloodhounds. In June 1642 two separate groups broke into the king's Waltham Forest. On the 23rd Francis Swift gentleman (son of Sir Francis), Edward Brazier turner, and Gerald Beech labourer killed a buck with a handgun. Then on the 29th, perhaps to go one better

> William Miller of Wormley butcher, Thomas Acres of Cheshunt, James and Phillip Shelley of Nazing gentlemen, together with 22 unknown malefactors about 11 in the morning broke in ... with mungrells and greyhounds and killed a redd deere worth 20s in the forest called Gallyhill and they riotously remained there until midnight of the same day.

Justice for Francis was indeed swift: little more than two weeks later he pleaded guilty at Chelmsford Quarter Sessions and was fined 10s, although there is no record that any of the others was punished.

Grand larceny was defined as the theft from a house of goods worth a shilling or more, and was punishable by death. In 1589, a labourer named Edward Hall was found guilty of stealing a sorrel gelding from William Glover of Glascocks and sentenced to hang. Strangers, second offenders and those lower down the social scale were less likely to find mercy; Richard Burbry came into all three categories. On 23rd March 1607, Burbry, a husbandman of Barking, was acquitted of breaking into a house there and stealing goods worth £5.8s. Only six weeks later Burbry, now described as a labourer of Nazeing, broke into the house of Lawrence Payson alias Pawson and stole a gold ring (6s), a gilt ring (18d), and a cambrick band with a gorget (3s). This time he was found guilty and sentenced to hang.

Such drastic action was, however, the exception. In 1564 another labourer, Richard Skragges, was accused of breaking into the close of Thomas Sayer and stealing a bay-bald gelding worth 56s 8d, but acquitted. In 1578 at Chelmsford Assizes the jury presented "John

Gebsson a bowt the age of xviij yeres being an ingnorant sempell fellow" for drawing his dagger in the churchyard "a mounske a compeny of madens", but he did not hurt any of them and so the jury asked that "he may have his coreckcyon with your lordships' faver".

The jury sometimes considered the crime as not worthy of the death penalty and found the accused guilty of petty larceny, even though the goods were worth more than a shilling. In 1583 Nicholas Sameswell, labourer, stole a bridle worth 10d from Henry Cramphorne and three aprons (18d) from William Goose but was convicted only of petty larceny to the value of 4d and 5d. Lettice Greygoose, who was probably only sixteen years old and came from a family which had several brushes with the law, was even luckier: in 1613 she burgled the house of Mary Cole and stole a petticoat worth 10s, a pair of stockings (1s), a neckerchief (6d) and 2 coifs (6d). Even though the goods were worth 12s she was convicted of petty larceny to the value of 10d and ordered to be whipped, an indication that she had neither goods to forfeit nor money to pay a fine.

Benefit of clergy was originally a privilege dating from the twelfth century and reaching its high point after the murder of Becket. Clergy accused of a crime could claim it and then be tried before a church court, where those convicted would receive a punishment much less severe than the King's Court would have imposed. The privilege came to be extended to any man who could read and, in the seventeenth century, even to women. Gradually, however, the situations in which mitigation of the punishment was permitted became restricted but benefit of clergy could still be claimed in cases, among others, where courts saw hanging as too serious a punishment. In 1580 John Symson, a husbandman, broke into the house of William Pygram and stole sheets worth 10s, 5 table napkins (3s 4d), several other pieces of linen (20s), and 4s 6d in money. In 1615 Thomas Darby stole from John Tey gentleman 3¾ yards of canvas (4s), a pitchfork (18d), a dagger (3s 4d), 2 pairs of stockings (4s), a pair of shoes (2s 6d), 2 towels (4s 6d), a pair of stockings (3s), and a handkerchief (1s). Both were found guilty but allowed benefit of clergy. Darby's status is not given but Symson, as a husbandman, would perhaps have been able to read and write, although even this may not have been a necessary qualification. In 1595 Elias Midson, a labourer, stole ten oxen worth £28 from Edward Greville Esq; few labourers, however, were literate and the winter of 1595 was exceptionally harsh, so the verdict may have reflected an elasticity of definition and a degree of compassion.

"The head-quarters of the Puritans"

The importance of religion in this period can scarcely be overestimated: "People are governed more by the pulpit than the sword in time of peace," commented King Charles I. Essex, being within easy reach of London, Cambridge and the Continent, was always open to new influences. The Reformation, inspired by such men as Luther, Calvin, and Tyndale, laid deep and lasting roots. Puritans were independent-minded thinkers who believed in social justice, strong parliamentary government, and the right to oppose authoritarianism in church and state. When they attained positions of power, however, they often demonstrated an authoritarian streak of their own. They saw the world as divided into sheep and goats, with themselves working on the side of God against evildoers, who could equally be Roman Catholics and high churchmen or thieves and drunkards. Such a doctrine was intrinsically divisive and Puritanism split most parishes in Essex, which was seen by the godly as "the place of most religion in the land" and by their opponents as "the first-born of parliament". According to William Winters, the local historian and Baptist preacher, the Nazeing Puritans "gathered at night for sacred and secret worship in the woody part of Galleyhill to escape the detection of their persecutors". By 1600, however, the village had become a stronghold for them.

Some indication of the spiritual state of the village can be gleaned from the careers of its vicars. After the dissolution of Waltham Abbey, the advowson went to the Crown and Nicholas Lock was appointed vicar of Nazeing. Shortly after the accession of Mary I he was dismissed for refusing to put away his wife and become a Catholic priest. Thomas Broke and Christopher Wall, both priests, were installed as his successors. Shortly after Mary's death, Elizabeth I appointed to the living Edward Hopkinson, described with the Protestant title of clerk and then, in 1571, she appointed John Hopkins. In 1583-4 he refused Archbishop Whitgift's demand that all clergy should accept royal supremacy, the Book of Common Prayer, and the Thirty-Nine Articles and, in 1589, he was deprived of the living for nonconformity. It is unlikely that the parishioners of Nazeing supported the dismissals of Lock and Hopkins, because in 1608, shortly after his appointment, Richard Sherman was charged with being "a great gamester" and for "his disordered preaching and railing most absurdly, to the great grief and offence of his congregation". Evidently their complaint was upheld because Sherman resigned.

Around the same time Benet Eliot moved with his family from the Hertfordshire village of Widford to Nazeing. He was wealthy enough to send his son John to Cambridge, where the young man was deeply influenced by a noted Puritan divine, Thomas Hooker. John Eliot returned to Nazeing but in 1631, unable to live with the increasingly restrictive rule of King Charles I and Archbishop Laud, sailed to the newly established colony of Massachusetts in America. There he was elected first minister of the church in the town of Roxbury. Generally the town is thought to have been named after a pile of rocks nearby but it is possible that as a boy Eliot lived at Ruxborowes, before Robert Keyes bought it, and named the new settlement after his old homestead.

John Eliot's greatest work began when he encountered the Indians and became the first English Protestant to preach the Gospel to native people. Eliot translated the Bible into several Indian languages but, unlike many Victorian missionaries, he accepted their culture and trained natives as his successors. He was heartbroken when, in 1675, war broke out between the settlers and the Indians. Bravely he risked the wrath of his fellow-Englishmen and lived to see the two parties reconciled. He died in 1690 and richly deserved his title of "Apostle to the Indians".

Eliot is remembered rightly as one of Nazeing's greatest sons, yet perhaps his effect on his home village was not an unmixed blessing. In successive migrations during the 1630s some 150 men, women, and children went from Nazeing to America, forming the nucleus of the Roxbury church. According to J.S. Stephens of Cheshunt College, Eliot's influence meant that

> Nasing was the head-quarters of the Puritans of the neighbourhood, and that they used to assemble at this village from miles around to worship God, and to plan for their safety.

Thus some of Eliot's followers were not born in the village. Nevertheless around one fifth of the inhabitants of Nazeing emigrated, among them representatives of old-established families such as Ruggles, Payson, Graves, Shelley, and Curtis (to which family there is a recent memorial in All Saints' Church). The restrictions on commoning and new building probably meant that for some people economic motives were as strong as religious ones. The emigration was the greatest single upheaval in Nazeing between the Black Death and the twentieth century.

Despite the losses the Puritan influence remained strong. Edward Jude, who had succeeded Richard Sherman as vicar, was a devout Puritan who presided over the "dismissal service" for the pilgrims. In his time

Ninnings, the home of William Campe, a Puritan elder in the 1640s. In 1662 he left it to his son, also William. From a photograph of around 1900.

the Vicarage constituted a house, garden, barn, and stables, as it did until after the Second World War, with seventeen acres adjacent and two in the mead. Jude stayed until 1640, when Robert Lewis was appointed by Charles I. Soon Lewis became the third Nazeing vicar to be ejected, but by the Parliamentarians for not being Puritan enough. He was succeeded by another in the line of Puritan Cambridge graduates, Jeremy Dyke, a prolific author who had previously been vicar of Epping. He was a cheerful spirit of whom it was said that "an ounce of mirth mixed with the same degree of grace will serve God more than a pound of grace". John Harper, vicar from 1643 to 1648, and the elders William Campe of Ninnings and John Ruggles carried out Puritan reforms within the parish. At the 1644 quarter sessions, for example, Ruggles gave evidence concerning Robert Sawall's unlicensed and unruly alehouse. In 1648 Harper moved in the opposite direction to his predecessor and became vicar of Epping

After the execution of Charles I the advowson passed by default to the lord of the manor, the Earl of Carlisle, but, as he was an absentee and a delinquent, the vicarage was sequestered and "in the hands of divers of the parishioners". This may indicate that Nazeing had a Leveller element similar to those in London, more radical and egalitarian than the propertied Parliamentarians who controlled the Commonwealth. In 1650 the parishioners employed Henry Albery as a temporary minister and "allowed him 10s on every Sabbath-day". Either this was not enough or his spiritual qualities were greater than his administrative ones because his keeping of the parish registers left much to be desired.

The lords of the manor versus the villagers

The early part of Queen Elizabeth's reign was a time of relative economic prosperity and social calm. By the 1590s, however, a combination of rapidly growing population and poor harvests brought about harder times so that conflict grew throughout England, culminating in the Civil War. It seems likely that in their later years the Waltham Abbey authorities became more lax and that the Dennys were preoccupied with other matters, so that the villagers of Nazeing took advantage of the opportunity to advance their position. When the business-like Sir Edward Denny came into his inheritance in 1590, his determined attempt to make his estates profitable coincided with the onset of the period of troubles. The stage was set for a series of disputes between the lords of the manor and their tenants who, by contrast with the lawless and riotous behaviour seen in many forest areas, generally chose legal and peaceful methods such as prosecutions and petitions. The conflict culminated in 1651, when the villagers won a famous victory over the 2nd Earl of Carlisle.

Denny seems to have acted in a high-handed manner from the outset. In 1598 the attorney-general, Sir Edward Coke, later a Chief Justice, who was the greatest lawyer of his age, began a series of actions against him over liberties, franchises, and property rights within the forests of Waltham Abbey and Nazeing. In these cases judgement was given in Denny's favour. Then, in 1603, a group of 33 Nazeing tenants took him to the Court of Chancery. Substantial citizens in the form of "Wm Cooke gen[tleman]" and Robert Porter "cler[gyman]" were supported by thirty other copyholders, including members of long-established families such as Campe, Shelley, Keyes, and Algar. It was a typical forest dispute over the ownership of timber and the highly prized right to cut it, which were of great economic importance to landlord and tenants. Both sides employed professional lawyers who, as was usual in such cases, searched the court rolls for precedents. "The decree for the Tennants of Nasinge" confirmed their right to "lopp, topp, shred, stock, fell, cutt downe, cary away, sell...or otherwise dispose of all manner of tymber trees and other trees woodes & underwoods whatsoever...", and Sir Edward Denny had to give in.

Twenty years later Denny paid the tenants back in kind, when he became suspicious that they were allowing strangers to graze stock on Nazeingwood Common. He instructed his men to drive the beasts into a pound and it was found that there were 1,200 sheep, whereas he said that there should have been only 600. The tenants entered Nazeing Wood, which despite their grazing rights was still Denny's private park, used for hunting. They cut down the pound, as they were by law entitled to do if they were left with insufficient common. When Denny took them to the Court of Star Chamber for pound-breach their defence was that they had freed the animals because they "were like to be much worse for the chasing, driving and impounding". It is curious that this was precisely the time when the jury was vigorously supporting restrictions on commoning. It may be that either those who broke down the fences were not the yeomen and master-craftsmen who provided the jury or that Denny and the tenants disagreed over the number of houses with common rights.

As the tensions which eventually culminated in the Civil War grew, there was a split between the Royalist gentry and the predominantly Puritan tenants. In 1626 Charles I pardoned Denny for his various highhanded actions towards the tenants, a move which can scarcely have endeared the king or the lord of the manor to them. Four years later Denny formally claimed the "perquisites and profits of Courts Leet and View of Frankpledge ... the Assize and Assay of Bread, Wine and Beer and the punishment and correction of the same". He asserted his jurisdiction not only over his own tenants but also over anyone residing in the half-hundred of Waltham.

The steward's papers show that the jury was willing to take on the rich and powerful as well as the poorer sort in defence of its precious common and other rights. A variable rate of fine for failure to attend the manorial court indicates that they differentiated according to social status and perhaps ability to pay:

> Item we Amerce the Tennants for not appearing at the cort; the gentlemen at three shillings apiece, the Yeomen at xii d a peice, the poor at ii d a peice.

Evidently Sir Francis Swift (owner of Harold's Park and Lodge Farm) encroached on the Common because, in 1637, the jury pained

> Sir ffrancis Swift to laye out the ground wch hee hath fenced in out of

Nasinge Wood & to pull upp his hedge there before Lammas Daye next upon payne to forfeyt if it be then unlayed out...£ xx.

The following year the jury made a similar pain and doubled the forfeit for non-compliance to forty pounds. This exceptionally high figure may represent the severity of the misdemeanour or Swift's wealth and unpopularity, although clearly forfeits increased if they were not acted upon.

Both James I and Charles I loved hunting and strengthened their control of the royal forests near London. In the 1630s, while ruling without Parliament, Charles developed an alternative source of income by fining anyone who encroached on the forest. This policy directly affected people dependent on the forest economy and must have increased the king's unpopularity. In 1641 he ordered a perambulation of Waltham Forest to establish its boundaries. It was found that Nazeing was part of the forest, although the tenants had common rights in Nazeing Wood and by the river.

When the Civil War broke out in 1642 these underlying tensions came to the surface. The Carlisles were divided over the issue: the Earl's family were staunch Royalists and his cousin George Goring was a leading Royalist general, but the Countess's father and brother were active Parliamentarians. Lucy Percy, James Carlisle's step-mother, seems to have been personally split over the war: she was a double agent, spying for both sides, and found herself in prison when she decided for the Royalists just before they were defeated. Although James himself felt it prudent to spend the Civil War out of

Lucy Percy, second wife of the 1st Earl of Carlisle, was described as one of the most beautiful women of her age. From a painting by Van Dyck.

the way in Barbados, Parliament nevertheless deemed him a delinquent and his estate was confiscated.

In 1643 Parliament sequestrated the land of 27 Nazeing owners, most of whom held the more substantial properties. Probably at least half of the land in the village was affected. William King had accumulated estates with an annual rental of £123 12s 6d, and there is evidence that his rapid rise and his Royalist sympathies had provoked a degree of malice: at the Quarter Session in 1642 he was presented for not repairing a footbridge below "Carseyes" leading to Broxbourne church and market but nine years later, when the Civil War was over and the Commonwealth had brought a degree of stability, the jury certified that "it was neither churchway, marketway nor millway but only to go out of one marsh into the other" and found it "very sufficiently made". William Shelley senior had land with an annual rental of £121 9s, Sir Richard

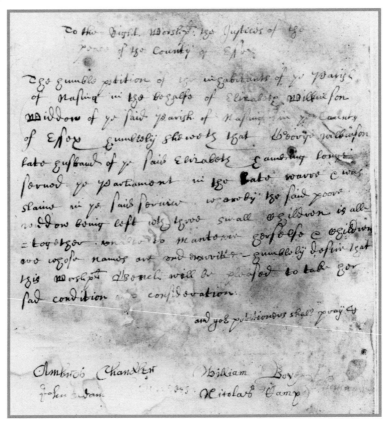

The 1653 petition by the inhabitants of Nazeing on behalf of Elizabeth Wilkinson, whose husband "having served ye parliament in the late warre & was slaine in ye said service".

Lucy of £93 3s 4d, and Sir Francis Swift of £53. It is curious that the groups which broke into the royal forest in 1642 included younger members of the Royalist Swift and Shelley families; perhaps they were hedging their political bets, unless they were just out for fun with youths of their own age. As well as Shelley, prominent Puritan names such as Campe, Curtis, and Payson appear among those whose property was sequestrated. This suggests that there were Royalists in Nazeing and that at this level too many families, like the Carlisles, were deeply divided.

Although there was a Royalist minority in Essex, it was a predominantly Parliamentarian county. Therefore the Civil War never came to Nazeing, although Nazeing men went to the war and some did not come back. The inhabitants, led by the Puritan churchwardens and overseers, addressed a petition to the Chelmsford Quarter Sessions on behalf of Elizabeth Wilkinson, whose husband "having long served the parliament in the late warr was slaine in the said service". Being left with three small children, "the said poor widdowe" was unable to maintain her family and the petitioners asked the bench to "take her sad condition into consideration".

In many places prosperous yeomen formed an alliance with the gentry but in Nazeing they remained resolutely on the side of those poor whom they saw as deserving, such as Elizabeth Wilkinson. In 1651 another petition to the Quarter Sessions brought the inhabitants into direct conflict with the lord of the manor. The language gives a real feel for the hardships of the villagers in this period. Its clarity can scarcely be improved upon, so it is worth quoting in full:

> Whereas about ten years since the parishioners, "by order of State", did erect a watch-house at their proper charges in Nazeing Wood, which was and yet is employed to that use, which about eight years after falling into great decay for want of thatching and daubing, one Nich. Wilkenson, being in the towne and utterly destitute of a dwelling offered to some of the neighbours to repair it and make it habitable and meet for a watch-house if they would suffer him to dwell therein, whereunto some consented and he repaired it and he hath ever since dwelt therein. Howbeit they are lately informed that he standeth indicted for the cottage by the Earl of Carliell lord of the manor of Nazeing, and forasmuch as the township is oppressed with many poor and have not housing wherein to bestow them, they now therefore beseech that the proceeding of the indictment be stayed until the next Quarter Sessions that in the meantime Wilkenson may procure friends to entreat the Earl of Carliell to order the withdrawal of the indictment and to suffer him to dwell therein during his life.

The petition was signed by eleven leading men of Nazeing and there is a note that the process was "stayed". Their emphasis on the fact that they had made the watch-house "by order of State" may suggest both continuing resentment of Charles's high-handedness and delicate political tact in dealing with the new Parliamentary regime.

The Earl of Carlisle had returned to England recently and was seeking to recover his Nazeing estate. The solidarity of the petitioners against his attempt to evict poor Nicholas Wilkenson demonstrated the weakness of his position and Carlisle made a unique settlement with the commoners, whereby he set aside for himself two fifty acre portions of the common, in addition to the forty acres of Greenmead which had been separated in the 1530s, and gave the remaining 414 to the commoners. Nazeing Wood was still an enclosed park, stocked with deer for hunting, so his giving up such a valuable piece of property represented a considerable victory for the commoners. In 1656 this was confirmed by an Act of Oliver Cromwell's Protectorate.

The uniqueness of Nazeingwood Common

Nineteenth century commentators noted that "the Common is a most peculiar common" and that "The case, perhaps, is singular". This is not because common rights are attached to certain properties, a situation which applies elsewhere, but because the common itself belongs to the owners of those properties rather than to the lord of the manor. Even after the Restoration minor Royalist supporters were seldom compensated for their losses during the Commonwealth. In any case the financial and dynastic chaos which followed Carlisle's death probably left his heirs too weak to pursue the issue. Samuel Wake Jones, who inherited the lordship of the manor in 1691, would scarcely have wished to overturn a settlement which was by then over thirty years old. Importantly, such a move would have been unlikely to find favour with the new regime of King William and Queen Mary. So the "singular case" has survived.

CHAPTER 4
"A SAD LAWLESS SET"
1660 to 1778

This was a period of comparative stability. The monarchy was restored in 1660 when King Charles II was crowned following the downfall of the Commonwealth. The religious dissension that started under Henry VIII continued. In about 1630 perhaps one in five people in Nazeing had felt sufficiently oppressed to leave the village for the uncertainty and hardship of the New World. The effective end of the Denny/Hay dynasty came at the time of the Restoration, bringing to Nazeing a period in which a strong lead was increasingly lacking. Whereas the villagers had stood together in a common cause under the Commonwealth, by the early years of George III they were being described as "a sad lawless set".

The effects of change

Nazeing was of course relatively close to London. Indeed information sources such as wills indicate that the village had closer connections with London than with the county town of Chelmsford. Nazeing had relatively good road links to the capital via nearby Epping, Waltham Abbey and Cheshunt. In addition, the River Lea provided good access because it ran into the Thames about three miles to the east of the City. The importance of the river can be seen from the improvements that were made in the 1760s, which led to the opening of the Lee Navigation designed by Smeaton and Telford in 1772.

Due to these connections, the plague in London during 1665 would have touched the villagers in various ways. One writer reported that it provoked many people to "pack up and leave London with all possible haste", so we may assume that a number passed through or stayed in Nazeing. They would not have been welcomed even by their close family and friends. Further trade with London would have been more difficult to find due to the fear of spreading the disease.

Many people would have sought a supernatural cause for the disaster and perhaps their feeling of doom was further confirmed when the plague was closely followed by the fire that devastated London in September

1666. Again this would have had a direct effect on village life, although the exact consequences are difficult to determine. As with the plague in the previous year, some homeless people would have moved to Nazeing, possibly returning to meet the need for labour to rebuild the city from the ashes. No doubt the opportunities were extensive for those who wished to leave the village to help rebuild London. This would have strengthened the associations between Nazeing and the capital.

The lords of the manor and Nazeing Bury

Sir Samuel Jones, the son of Isaac who had lent money to Lord George Goring, was a successful businessman, like his father. He was able to afford to buy Courteenhall in Northamptonshire for about £9,000. Being childless, in 1670 he made a will in favour of his nephew, Samuel Pierrepoint. Due to the "idle and unprofitable life" of Pierrepoint, the will was changed in favour of Samuel, the infant son of Sir William Wake and his own great nephew, on condition that he changed his name to Jones. The child inherited the estate on Sir Samuel Jones's death in 1672. The astute executors managed to obtain control of the Carlisle estates as they paid off the Goring and Carlisle debts. Thus, when Samuel Wake Jones came of age in 1691, he was the possessor of a considerable tract of land in Waltham Abbey and Nazeing. He lived at Waltham Abbey and took an active interest in Nazeing, as did his nephew and heir, Charles. In 1739, however, on the succession of Charles's nephew, also Charles, the family moved permanently to Courteenhall and left the Abbey House to fall into ruins. In 1747 he succeeded to the baronetcy but eight years later he died, without children, ending the Wake-Jones line. The title and estates were inherited by another branch of the Wake family, whose connection with Nazeing continues in titular form, the present lord of the manor being Sir Hereward Wake, the fourteenth baronet.

In 1671 the leading inhabitant was Edward Russell, godson of the 2nd Earl of Carlisle and the nephew of Carlisle's widow Margaret. He was the only blood relative of the lords of the manor ever recorded as actually resident in Nazeing. He was living at Green Mead Lodge because he happened to like the place. This was a substantial house near Lodge Farm which he probably held too.

Meanwhile Nazeing Bury was let to tenants. A court leet in 1669 recorded William North and James Payson as the occupants. Indeed, Nazeing Bury seems to have had two occupants over a long period. For example, in 1637, the court rolls mention John Payson and William Shelley and in 1721 Randall Lawrence and Richard Plummer. Thus at this time either Nazeing Bury had two occupants or it was two properties. In the eighteenth century there were certainly two properties because sometimes Nazeing Bury is referred to as the Great Bury and there is evidence of another property called the Little Bury. The court records of 1738 describe the occupants as "Randal Lawrance living in the Great Bury and Thomas Want living in the little Bury" and in 1750 there is a record of "John Lake occupying Nazeing Great Bury and Thomas Want occupying Nazeing Little Bury".

It now seems fairly certain that the Little Bury was situated very close to Nazeing Bury itself, although the nineteenth century Essex historian D.W. Coller had suggested that its location was either not known or situated elsewhere. Similarly, the Little Bury has sometimes been described as a manor. Again this is incorrect, as a true manor would have had held its own courts baron to deal with copyhold property but clearly the Nazeing manor courts had jurisdiction over the Little Bury. In the case of the Little Bury the term "manor" seems to be used loosely to describe an estate. The churchwardens' accounts indicate that by about 1772 the Little Bury building had disappeared and that its land was being farmed from Nazeing Bury. For example in both 1772 and 1780 John Lake of Nazeing Bury farmed 168 acres and about 35 acres of "Litel Berry" land; then between 1784-6 and 1795, James Goodwin of Nazeing Bury farmed 168 acres and 41 acres of "Little Bury Land".

Village life

Nazeing continued as a small farming community throughout this period. The size of its population and the way they led their lives seem to have remained relatively constant, despite what was going on in London and elsewhere in the country. The population, at about 550 persons, was much smaller than it is today and remained smaller than it had been in 1300. There were only about 120 houses and a similar number of farming units. People would have known one another due to the relatively small population of the village through the community activities, such as religious worship, in which they took part. Apart from exceptional events such as the Great Fire of London, few villagers would have travelled far for work or other purposes. Most people would have been involved in farming the land, although a small number are described in their wills as having other occupations such as shoe making and shop keeping. We can see from the churchwardens' accounts for this period that each farmer occupied land with an area of between one and perhaps a hundred and fifty acres but a fairly typical size would have been about twenty acres. In addition, the 98 houses with rights over Nazeingwood Common gave their occupants the use of common land grazing.

For perhaps a century until 1730, the number of farming units in Nazeing appears to have been relatively stable at about a hundred, a figure that is understandably very similar to the number of houses with the advantages of common rights. From 1730 the number steadily fell reflecting a move towards larger farms. The impact of this was amplified at the end of the century by the land purchases that were being made by a small number of families. Thus the number of farms seems to have been reduced to perhaps seventy-five in 1800. The major cause of this change was the increased land area that the yeoman farmers took on as tenants of the landowners, whereas the lot of the husbandmen and labourers was relatively unchanged.

The power that the inhabitants had shown in obtaining the 1651 settlement became weakened as land in Nazeing came to be owned by people outside the village. Their main interest was in collecting rents so that they had no direct interest in Nazeingwood Common. As they tended to be appointed trustees under the 1656 Act, the common fell into decay. Due to the lack of a suitable method to achieve change, in 1775 the seven surviving trustees signed an indenture to transfer ownership to eleven new trustees, of whom only the Reverend Thomas Salt, William Palmer, and John Banks paid rates to the church that year. The management of the common land was proving difficult and the owners received little benefit from it, so that there was seen to be a need for a replacement Act. Although we cannot be certain of their motives, perhaps we should not be surprised that it was William Palmer, who was building up his land holdings in Nazeing, who promoted the Act through Parliament in 1778.

Roads and tracks

As we would expect, the roads and tracks gave access around the village and to the four main centres of village life. Firstly, there was All Saints' Church in Upper Nazeing, where most of the villagers would attend at least one of the services each Sunday. Secondly there was Nazeing Bury in Lower Nazeing, where the courts of the lord of the manor were held. Lastly, there were the two main areas of common

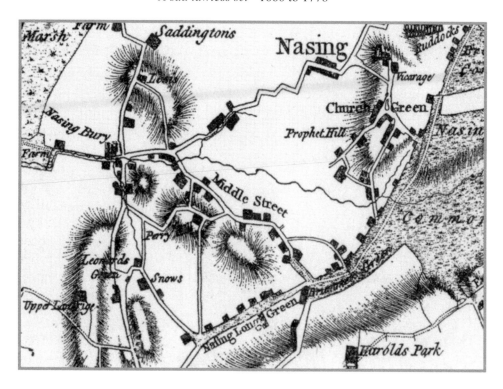

**Part of Chapman & André's 1777 map showing a road network that is
recognisable in today's highways, bridleways and footpaths.**

grazing, Nazeingwood Common in the east of the parish and the meads
beside the River Lea.

The first detailed map of Essex was published in 1777 by Chapman
and André. In addition to the above enlargement, the Nazeing part is
reproduced inside the front cover of this book. As may be seen, most of
the main roads were in the same position as they are today, although their
general condition would have been similar to today's farm tracks.

In addition to the principal roads, there were still many ancient
tracks, which gave access to the patchwork of fields which were the main
source of income and employment. As the villagers of Nazeing were
fairly widely scattered around the parish, most of them would have had to
walk a considerable distance to reach the church, which is only a field's
width from the northern boundary of the parish. Similarly, many lived a
long way from Nazeing Bury, sited to the west of the village, and yet
further from the mead land which provided valuable summer grazing. A
map produced in 1767 to show the lord of the manor's Nazeing estate
shows Nazeing Bury immediately adjacent to a field called West Field,
which was on the edge of the village next to the marsh.

The Manor Courts

The manor courts continued to be of great importance to the social structure of the village so, although his steward presided over them, the departure of their nominal head would not have been without significance.

Under the 1656 Act, Nazeing Wood or Nazeing Park was administered in the manor courts, as were common lands such as Nazeing Mead and Nazeing Marsh. We are fortunate that many of Nazeing's records of importance, those of the church and the manor courts, are still in existence. There is a continuous series of Manor Court Rolls from

The last Court Leet held for the Lord of the Manor Sir Hereward Wake at Nazeing 8th July 1925 under the Court Maple near the Church.

Standing: Mr Weare, unknown, Mr Pegrum, Mr Sinclair, Mr Cook, Mr Graham, Mr Crowe, Mr Nicholls, Mr Fowler, Mr Pulham, Mr Frogley. Seated: Mr Salway, Mr Reynolds, Mr Moore, Mr Jessopp (steward), Mr Mansfield, Mr Smith.

These were among the leading men in the village. Successive members of the families of some of them had attended the manorial courts for centuries.

1669 to 1913, apart from the period from 1735 to 1760, which have been lost. Coupled with the churchwardens' accounts and those of the Overseers of the Poor, mentioned later, these provide much information about the four main centres of life in Nazeing and about the people who lived or owned property in the village.

Because farmers typically rented their farms from landlords who usually lived outside the village, only a small proportion of land was worked by its owners. In the preceding chapter we saw how the manor courts were able to charge what appears today to be an unreasonably large fine when copyhold property changed hands, even within a family. Certainly these high fines, which some new owners could not afford, were one of the reasons for a gradual decline in the number of small landowners, who sold out to the large landlords. The concentration of land in their ownership reached its zenith in Nazeing during the nineteenth century. Clearly such a system would be unacceptable unless the copyhold tenants thought they had no option but to accede to it. It drifted on for another 200 years but during that time some copyholders bought out the lord of the manor's rights. Eventually the Copyhold Act of 1894 gave everyone the freedom to do so. A further Act in 1922 abolished the copyhold system entirely and, since all their other responsibilities had already been removed, the last of Nazeing's manor courts took place in 1925.

Despite the power that the lord of the manor was able to exert, the inhabitants, as copyholders and commoners, asserted themselves through their representatives at the lord of the manor's courts, where they lost few opportunities to restate that the occupants of Nazeing Bury did not have common rights. As Nazeing Bury was owned by the lord of the manor and the manor courts were held there, we can imagine the rather disrespectful scene when, as usually happened, this item was raised as the second one on the agenda, immediately after the election of the court's officers. Even though the lord of the manor did not live at Nazeing Bury and left the administration of the manor courts to his steward, the prominence of this particular edict (as in the example shown on page 78) says much more than the recorded words convey.

As an example of what the manor courts dealt with, the following text from 1738 is fairly representative. Until 1733 the court records were written in Latin so this is an early example following the introduction of English, which had become the official language of record.

The original spelling and general form have been retained in this transcript, although the text has been abbreviated and punctuation, which is non-existent in the original document, has been added to improve clarity. The "Leet" was a court where social rather than criminal misdemeanours were dealt with and the "Homage" was a group of the manor's tenants who were sworn in to form a jury to hear the various cases that were presented to them.

The Manor of Nazeing in the County of Essex

> The Court Leet and Court Baron of Charles Jones Esquire Lord of the said Manor there held upon Wdnesday the twenty fourth Day of May in the Eleventh year of the Reign of our Sovereign Lord George the second by the grace of God of Great Britain, France and Ireland King Defender of the faith and so forth and in the year of our Lord One Thousand Seven hundred and Thirty Eight before Andrew Searle Esquire Steward there.

The presentments of the Court Leet

It is Ordered by the Homage That

[Rights] Randal Lawrance living in the Great Bury and Thomas Want living in the Little Bury, the Dwellers and Landholders of Nazeing Lodge, the Dwellers and Landholders of Nazeing Vickridge shall not common in Nazeing Wood nor any of our commons upon pain to forfeit for every time so taken forty shillings

[Limits] no man shall put upon Nazeing Wood above the number of four Great Cattell and Twenty Sheep and a Ram, [nor] upon our Commons any Maingey or Farsey [another disease] horse nor any other diseased horse or colt upon pain to forfeit for every time so taken tenn shillings

no Man shall put upon our Commons any Hoggs or Piggs unringed upon pain to forfeit for every time so taken six pence a head

no Man shall take in any Inmate [outsider] upon pain to forfeit forty shillings a Month so long as they continue them Inmates

no Batchelor shall common upon any of our commons unless he be a householder upon to forfeit for every time so ofending forty shillings

no Man shall into any horse or colt unless he be fourteen hands high nor any stears into any of our commons upon pain to forfeit for every time so taken tenn shillings a head

We present

[Stud]   that our custom is to have a Bull and Bore and a Stallion kept at Nazeing Great Bury at the Charge of the Lord of the Manor for the use of the Tenants of Nazeing

[Tythes]   our custom for our parsonage for our corn the tenth for our grass two pence an acre

[General]   that no man shall take in any cattell that are not properly his own and them to have his mark on them to common in any of our commons upon pain to forfeit for every time so taken tenn shillings a head

[Fishing]   our custom is to fish in the Navigable River in Nazeing Mead and the Middle River in Nazeing Marsh

[Fines] Eadey Adams Widow for keeping a mangey colt upon Nazeing Wood if not taken off by Friday next upon a forfeit of tenn shillings

Thomas Want for laying dung in the highway by West field Gate that the surveyor cannot mend the highway if not removed by midsumer next upon pain a forfeit of forty shillings

Edward Camp and Henry Parkings for not making their ditches against Longfield Springs if not made by midsumer next upon a forfeit of forty shillings

Edward Hunt for not cutting his bushs and making his ditch against Brambell Croft leading to Madlands if not done by the tenth of June next upon a forfeit of forty shillings

The work of the Court Leet concluded with the appointment of two constables and two pindars, one each for Nazeing Common and Nazeing Meads. Similar appointments were made until the 1778 Act required the trustees to appoint a permanent pindar. The Leet thus dealt with the basic administrative functions of the community.

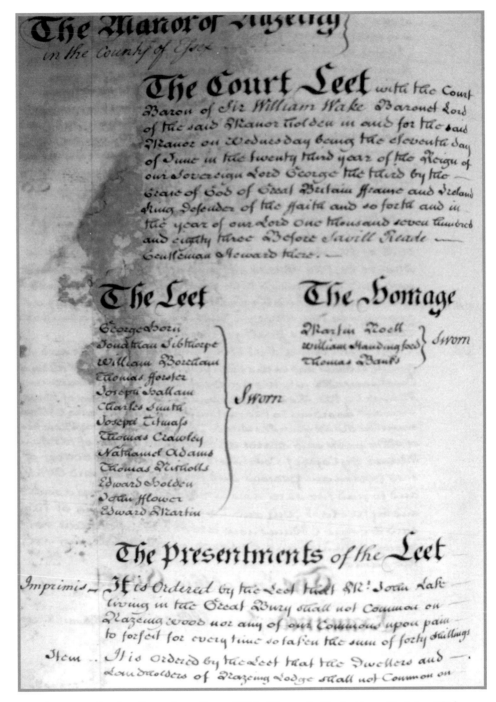

An example of a Court Leet from 1783. Towards the bottom, it states "It is ordered by the Leet that Mr John Lake living in the Great Bury [Nazeing Bury] shall not Common on Nazeing wood nor any of our Commons upon pain to forfeit … the sum of forty shillings".

The Manour of
Mazeing in the County
of Essex.

Whereas yesterday that is to
say the Twenty sixth day of May in the year of our Lord
One Thousand Seven hundred and Thirty Seven Elizabeth
Boalch a Widow and Relict of Thomas Boalch deceased
out of the Customary Tenants of the said Manour did
out of Court Surrender into the hands of Charles
Jones Esq. Lord of the said Manour by the Rodd by his
hands and Acceptance of Andrew Searle Esq. Steward
of the said Manour according to the Custom of the
same Manour All That Messuage or
Tenement called Perry Hill with the Barns Stables
Orchards Gardens Outhouses and Appurtenances
thereunto belonging containing by Estimation
Two Acres more or less And all that Close or parcell
of Land called a Ketherdown containing by Estimation
three Acres more or less and all That Close or parcell
of Land called upper Bowers containing by Estimation
Two Acres more or less and all That Close or parcell
of Land called a Riddy field containing by Estimation
Seven Acres more or less and all That Close or parcell
of Land called Seed Coops containing by Estimation
Six Acres more or less and all That Close or parcell of
Land called Wilkins Hill containing by Estimation
four Acres more or less and Common of pasture for
Eight Cows in a certain Common Marsh called
Mazeing Marsh which said Messuage Lands
Common of pasture and premisses are holde of the
Manour aforesaid by Copy of Court Roll by the
yearly Rent of fourteen Shillings and Eleven pence

Boalch's Surrender

Quittent
J.?
14. 11

Part of a Court Baron from 1737 in which "Elizabeth Boalch Widow … did …
surrender … All That Messuage or Tenement called Perry Hill …".

Land and Property

Land and property were usually described by either their owner or occupier rather than by their names. Where property names, such as Ninnings, Burnt Hall, and Wheelers, were recorded during the late seventeenth century, they show the continuity from the late Middle Ages to the present day. That many properties did not have names gives us an indication of how well people tended to know one another; this, along with the comparative permanence of field boundaries, appears to have been sufficient for precise identification of most houses. As owners acquired additional land to create farms, so the houses themselves acquired names for easier identification. This process continued until the general postal service made it necessary for all properties to be named or numbered.

The first detailed maps of Nazeing were not drawn until the second half of the eighteenth century. In 1765 the lord of the manor commissioned a map of his Nazeing estate and in 1777, following a survey in 1774, Chapman and André published their very accurate and detailed map which shows most of the roads and dwellings that were in existence at that time.

The following example from 1738 is fairly representative of the Court Baron's procedures for the transfer of copyhold land. Typically the initial surrender of land in accordance with a will took place in two main stages. The first was when the will was made and the relevant text was recorded in an abbreviated form at the subsequent Court Baron. Subsequently, when the owner had died, a fuller version of his surrender and the admittance of the new owner were incorporated. The following transcription relates to a piece of land called Napsies, which is part of a large field situated a short distance to the north of the house at Curtis Farm. This transfer shows how the owners of property tended to live further and further from the village.

> At This Court, it is found and presented by the Homage that upon the Twelfth Day of ... May, William Young one of the Customary Tenants of the said Manor did out of Court Surrender into the hands of the Lord [of the Manor] by the Rodd by the hands and Acceptance of John Windus Gentleman Deputy Steward ..., according to the Custom of the said Manor, All that close of pasture ground called ... Napsies containing by estimation three acres ... abutting South upon the Lands belonging to the poor of Cheshunt and North East on the Land ... of Robert Hughes Gentleman and common of pasture for six cows in the common marsh of Nazeing ... To the only use and Behoof of Catherine Dewe of Lamberhurst in the County of

Kent Spinster … Now at this Court came the said Catherine Dewe by Joseph Parnell her … Attorney and humbly Desired to be admitted Tenant to the said premises … To which said Catharine Dewe by her said Attorney the Lord of the Manor … in full and open Court did deliver seisin thereof by the Rodd according to the custom of the said Manor. To have and to hold the said close of land, common of pasture … with the Appurtenances thereunto belonging. To the only use and behoofe of … Catherine Dewe her heirs and assigns forever. To be holden of the Lord [of the Manor] by the Rodd … according to the Custom of the said Manor paying therefore yearly to the said Lord … the Annual Rent of four pence and doing performing such services and customs as have heretofore been used to be done … She gave to the Lord such Fine as appears in the Margin [£7.10s] and was admitted tenant thereof.

We do not know whether the land was purchased or bequeathed but other sources tell us that Catherine Dewe and her sisters Mary and Ann became major owners of property in Lamberhurst and elsewhere in Kent, Sussex, Hertfordshire, and in Essex at Nazeing. Their Nazeing property included Greenleaves and Darmers, which they probably inherited from their maternal grand-father, Francis Butler. Unfortunately, these properties are examples of freehold properties; not being copyhold they were not mentioned in the court records. Francis Butler was a resident of London but his will, dated 1721, shows his local connection to be that he

Goodalls from a photograph of around 1900. The house was rebuilt in about 1720. In the eighteenth century it was owned by the trustees of the Poor of Cheshunt. John Delamare was the customary tenant in his capacity as a trustee.

came from Roydon, where he wished to be buried "in or near the Grave of my deceased wife".

We should note also the size of the fine for admittance, which, at £7.10 shillings, seems rather hefty for a three acre piece of land, bearing in mind that the area of the occupied land in the village was about 2,400 acres in total. This indicates how such fines would have been a useful addition to the income of the lord of the manor, who would have put little back into the village.

If the rightful heir could not be located, the court would make three announcements to this effect. If no one came forward, the property would revert to the lord of the manor. Even then, as was the case with Goodalls during 1795, when the rightful heir eventually came forward, he was admitted as customary tenants upon payment of the fine. In this particular case, the former customary tenant was John Delamare, who was admitted in his capacity as a trustee of the Poor of Cheshunt. The customary tenancy, however, passed to "Elizabeth the wife of Peter Nouaille of Great Ness in the County of Kent Esquire [who] is the only Sister and next heir" rather than to one of the other trustees.

The continuing influence of nonconformity

Clearly the manor exerted significant authority over the people but there was also considerable religious influence and almost everyone attended at least one service each Sunday. All Saints', in Nazeing Upper Town, would have continued as the main centre for religious activity but, with continuing conflict between the denominations, a substantial proportion of the population began to attend services elsewhere led by nonconformist ministers. The dissenters tried to change the Church of England from within until their consciences forced them to reject the form of public worship decreed by the Act of Uniformity of 1662.

The consequences were enormous because about 2,000 clergymen throughout the land refused to comply. They were compelled to resign and thus "abandoned their snug vicarages and comfortable rectory-houses, and went forth, voluntarily embracing a life of hardship and poverty". Their congregations often followed these clergymen to other places of worship despite the threat of excommunication by the established church. Joseph Browne had been Nazeing's vicar for only five years when he left in 1663. He and his wife were listed as dissenting

Christians who, with twenty Nazeing residents, were excommunicated at the Archdeacon's visitation for not going to the parish church to worship.

The table below shows the Nazeing residents who were excommunicated in 1663, linked with information from the 1662 Hearth Tax and other sources. From this we can see that eighteen households were affected directly out of the 105 households listed in the Hearth Tax. Further, since most of these people came from families that had lived in Nazeing for very many years, we can infer that virtually every household in the village would have had close relatives, friends, or neighbours who were excommunicated. In addition, since the Hearth Tax tells us that over fifty per cent of homes in Nazeing had two hearths or fewer, those excommunicated were clearly an influential group.

Nazeing residents excommunicated in 1663

Name	Hearths*	Home
Joseph Browne and his wife	5	The Vicarage
Samuel and Mary Adams	3	Possibly Shottendens, Pecks Hill
John Augar [Algar]	2	Probably Warleys / Feltre, Middle St.
Thomas Bezill [Bassell]	3	Not known. Possibly later at Darmers
Ambrose & Joh. Chandler	3	Not known but later at Gardner's
Edward Daniell	3	Probably Tatsfords, Nazeing Rd
John Fosner [? Foscue]	3	J Foscue probably Burnt Hall, Middle St.
Robert Hawdon		Not known
Robert Hockley	2	Possibly The Rayles (loc. unknown)
William Hubbins [Hobbins]	1	Not known
William and Dorothy North	8	Nazeing Bury
Thomas Peacocke		Probably Callis House, Bumbles Green
John Pegrum	1	Possibly The Hole in Upper Town
John Reade	3	Probably Lukes in Upper Town
Jn. Riggles [Ruggles] sen. & wife	3	Mottes/Walnut Tree Cottage, Middle St.
Johnn Riggles [Ruggles] junior	2	Not known
Ingold [? John] Shelley	2	Parkers, Hoe Lane (John Shelley)
Thomas Shelley		Probably Greenleaves, Hoe Lane

* Taken from the 1662 Hearth Tax list

Joseph Browne's departure would have been a great disappointment to the village's common people, who would have seen it as further interference in their lives by the establishment. That so many prominent villagers refused to conform, despite the consequences of doing so, shows the great strength of nonconformist views in Nazeing at this time. Thus, we can see that in the 1660s many of Nazeing's villagers were still prepared to suffer for their religious beliefs, as had their forefathers who set off for the New World in the 1630s.

As a consequence of this strength of feeling, the established church found that its congregations preferred to follow the ejected nonconformist ministers to services conducted away from the parish churches. An Act was passed which prohibited separate congregations and forbade dissenting clergy from being within five miles of any place where they had preached previously. Joseph Browne had opened a school and stayed in the Nazeing area as a nonconformist minister until this became unlawful according to the Five Mile Act of 1665.

Despite the Act, it seems that Browne returned to Nazeing after a few years and, presumably for some act of nonconformity, was fined a sum that he could not pay. As a result, the contents of his house were confiscated. The villagers persuaded him to stay but a warrant was issued for his arrest and, for the second time, his property was at risk. Browne was forewarned by the Justice of the Peace's gardener who had overheard the conversation. Thus he fled in the night at a few hours' notice with whatever goods he and his family could carry. Eventually he went to live in London and did not return to Nazeing until 1690, when greater religious freedom came with the passing of the Toleration Act in the wake of the Glorious Revolution. Clearly the long-term religious problems had not reduced Browne's love of Nazeing and its people because, after ministering to his followers for another decade, he chose to be buried at All Saints', in 1700.

Despite the restrictions that existed for a century afterwards, nonconformist worship continued in secret but with precautions being taken to avoid discovery. The Toleration Act of 1689 allowed more openness by nonconformist religious groups, so that many congregations were established by dissenting ministers throughout the country. In 1697 the house of Robert Pirley, who lived in Nazeing, was registered by Joseph Landy as a Baptist place of worship. Then, in 1701, the house of James Person was registered by Christopher Carlisle as a Presbyterian meeting house. As Joseph Browne had died in 1700, James Person may well have taken over his work in the village.

It is possible that John Wroth took action against other nonconformists, since John Chandler's Account as All Saints' Overseer of the Poor in 1701 records expenditure "for 5 journeys to Mr Wroth about Thomas Chawkley", a name synonymous with nonconformity in Nazeing during the first half of the eighteenth century. The churchwardens' accounts indicate that there were two Thomas Chalkleys, presumably father and son, who are recorded as occupiers of land in Nazeing from the 1670s until about 1750. Thomas Chalkley junior was minister of Harlow Baptist Church but, from 1712 until his death in 1750, he held services every Sunday in his house in Nazeing. He was a major landholder, occupying about eighty acres from around 1710 until the 1740s. Although the house has not been identified for certain, the most likely property is Newmans Farm (now Felsteads), which was owned subsequently by Thomas Chalkley's descendants, Isaac Gould and the Reverend Gould, and, in 1824, by a Mr Chalkley Gould.

Thomas Chalkley was clearly a strong influence because in 1715 the Baptist Church of "Nazeing, Harlow and Looton [either Loughton or Latton]" was said to have a congregation of 500. As the population of Nazeing also was around 500 people, this would have reduced significantly the attendance at All Saints' where, in 1735, the second service each Sunday was cancelled because "they will not come in the afternoon"

After Thomas Chalkley's death in 1750 nonconformist services may have continued for a while in Nazeing but they had ceased by 1766. Several Baptists were still known to be in the parish, although their numbers were said to be on the decline.

Marsh-Mallows & oile of St John's Wort for Onion's daughter.

Despite the conflict within the Church throughout this period, All Saints' was the only option for baptism, marriages, and funerals. In 1755 the Marriage Act made it illegal for marriages to take place other than in church. Indeed the Church of England must, in many ways, have retained a position at the heart of the community despite the dissension by those who, in other circumstances, would have attended its services at All Saints'. In particular, and to demonstrate its central role, there were two pairs of church appointees who had responsibility for collecting money from all the occupiers of land in the village. These were the churchwardens and the Overseers of the Poor, both of whom were elected annually until 1803.

Both the churchwardens and the Overseers of the Poor produced accounts of their income and expenditure. Most of these accounts from the 1660s until 1800 are still in existence and are a major source of information on the village throughout this period. The accounts of income include complete annual lists of the occupiers of land and either the acreage that they occupied or the rate that was charged, from which the number of acres can be calculated. The accounts of expenditure give very precise information on how the money was spent and so provide an insight into the needs and costs of the time.

The churchwardens collected money that was used for costs directly incurred on the church building itself. For example, in 1690 and in 1691 the accounts show that they paid one shilling "for mending ye Church door key", 1s.4d for "ye Church door lock", 2s "for two years Regesters", 6s "for mending ye bells", 5s "for glaysing ye church windows" and 1s "for leather for ye bells". Sums were paid regularly "for relieving passengers which came ... with a pass" so it appears there was a system for providing basic aid to some travellers. William Feast, a churchwarden, had to travel to Romford, where he was sworn in and regularly attended court.

Despite the income received by the churchwardens the vicarage needed to be rebuilt in 1738 after being allowed to lapse into a state of disrepair. In 1765 a sundial inscribed with its latitude (51 degrees 32 minutes) was fitted on the stair turret at All Saints'

Many of the disbursements by the Overseers of the Poor were in the form of either single or regular payments to provide the needy with the basic necessities of food, shelter, clothes, and warmth. Each month, about twenty people typically received support. Some payments were for unspecified purposes "in their time of need" but it seems to have been more normal for a specific purpose to be named. For example, in 1692 1s 6d was paid "to goode Bentley for looking to the Wid Knight when she was sick" and, following her death, they paid 8s "for a coffin to bury the Wid Knight in" and a further 8s "for bread & cheese & drink at her Buriall". Clothes such as shoes and shirts were often paid for but in 1693 they paid 10s "for a hatt & shues & stockings & shirts for Oliver Simson". The Simson boys were helped for a few years and we can see from the 1692 account that their mother had been widowed. The 1694 account shows that she had probably died because Widow Wright was paid £3 4s to keep one of the Simson boys for a year. At this time a pair of shoes cost about 2s 6d for a boy and 4s for a man; a shirt cost from 1s to 2s 6d, stockings about 8d. Oliver Simson was helped again with a full set of clothes at 16s 10d. A year's rent appears to have cost between 16s and £2 10s; we should bear in mind that this was paid to the needy, who were likely to be in the cheaper property.

Some payments may seem to us to be for obscure purposes but, no doubt, they were deemed to be of sufficient importance to be paid for out of the funds for the poor. For example, in 1711, one shilling was "Paid for Marsh-Mallows & for oile of St John's Wort for Onion's daughter".

The lists of payments leave us with an impression of a caring community where those that were able felt an obligation to help those who were not. They were even willing to help those in distress who were not in any way associated with the village such as those who lived in distant parts. This found practical expression through special collections, recorded in the church registers. For example, in 1689 a collection made when £3 "was gathered for the releife of much distressed Protestants of Ireland". Yet even collections of this kind raised strong feelings because in 1690 "by reasen of y[e] present neccsary taxes w[hi]ch are heavy upon our Parish wee then cause why these following Breeze [Briefs] cant now be collected or any moneys given to them".

The following extracts are from the Accounts of the Overseers of the Poor at All Saints':

		£	s	d
1692	for 2 dayes of my self stacking of faggots & one day removing of the Widow Simsons goods & Carting out wood to the poor		3	0
1693	paid to Richard Dennish for Isaac Haldings house rent	2	10	0
	given to Sam Pecock to buy him some wood		18	0
	given to mother Bentley to buy her a wheele		3	6
	given to John Morrell when he was lame		3	0
1694	paid for A Coffin for Walls Child		3	0
	paid for burying the Wid Burton		7	0
	paid for an order to carry away Tho Simons		2	6
c1702	given to Hen. Wilkinson Junr some Cole		5	0
	paid goodwife Keyes & goodwife Hale for laying out Widow Chandler		2	0
	given to Robert Carter towards Cloathing his Children		6	0
	for the Clarks fees for the Burying of Tho Peggram		3	4
	given to goodwife Scott for looking to Tho. Peggram Senr when he was sick		2	0
1706	Paid to Stephen Green for half a yeares Rent for the widow Grave …		12	6

Paid to Thomas Chawkley for faggotts for the poor		1	10	0
Given to James Scott for the mending his shoes			1	6
Paid to Water Clemenshaw with James Mathews				
Being his prentice & binding & Expenses				
& my Journey to Hodsdon [Hoddesdon]		5	7	6
Paid to William Bancock for keeping a bastard Child				
of Eliz Norths 2 weeks			4	0
Paid to Daniel Exsall for keeping Martha Boultons				
bastard Child 12 Months at 6s a Month		3	12	0
Paid to James Marshall for keeping Nicholas Graves				
children 17 weeks & for mending their shoes		5	16	2
Paid for Mary Rickards petticoat & the making of it			5	1
Paid for a Horse & man to carry Elizabeth Grave to				
the Doctor's			2	2
1712	Laid out for cloaths for the widdow Bentlies son at			
	his going to service		5	0
1716	spent when we took Antney Trayhorn & for mareying		14	6
	for my Jorney to Chesen [Cheshunt] at the sametime		2	0
	paid to Wid Physicke for 4 monthes at 2s a month for			
	hous Rent for bek Peggran		8	0
	paid to John Lawrance for a years Rent dew in January			
	the 23 day for the wid Laraner		16	0

In addition to this kind of assistance to the needy, there were other schemes to provide relief to the poor. For example, in 1693 the vestry ordered that pauper children should "be bound apprentice" as they previously had. As early as 1637 the steward's papers record that a farmer was presented for "not sufferinge the water to have the right course from the Wholve [culvert] by the Almeshouses". It is possible that this was near the King Harold's Head, on the same site as the almshouse sold by the parish two hundred years later, although there is no reference to it in the intervening period and the identification is far from certain. In 1637 there is mention of the parish poorhouse, described in 1698 as being situated on Church Green. This was almost certainly the present-day Ricketts and it remained in use until 1796.

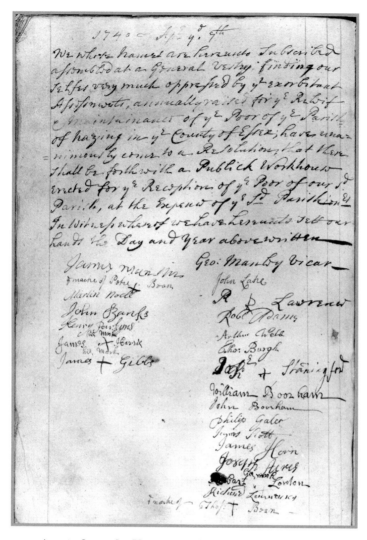

**A note from the Vestry meeting in 1740 that decided
"that there shall be forthwith a Publick Workhouse
erected for ye Reception of ye Poor …". It was signed by
23 leading villagers, including the vicar George Manley.**

Almshouses and poorhouses were usually a shelter for the elderly and infirm, whereas workhouses were intended to provide the able-bodied poor with productive employment. An Act of 1722 authorised parishes to establish their own workhouses, and in 1740 the vestry decided that a workhouse should be built to control the costs of poor relief because there had been complaints from the parishioners that they were "oppressed by the exorbitant assessments annually raised for relief and maintenance of the poor". However, the vestry's decision was not acted upon in full

Longyard Cottage, probably the workhouse in the mid 18th century.

because the house and field of William Ricketts was bought and a quit rent paid in 1742. Probably the house was used as a workhouse for a short period for in 1743 it was recorded that "tis agreed between the Officers of Nazeing & Richard Lawrence ... that the said Richard Lawrence is to give to thee Work-House six pounds ten shillings per year". In 1753, however, the Churchwardens' Accounts referred to rent paid by "Wm Jennings for Workhouse". The property is probably Longyard Cottage, where Jennings and his family continued to live for many years.

Richard Lawrence lived at Darmers from about 1733 to 1776. He was a descendant of Randall Lawrence, who had occupied Nazeing Bury at the beginning of the century and seemed prone to charitable acts because the accounts for 1749 show "Rich.d Lawrence joynttly with his Son Randall bond for a Female Bastard of Millicent Parkys".

As this incident indicates, although there was a considerable number of people who suffered from poverty, assistance was given within the community by private charity and by help from friends and neighbours, as well as through the Poor Law. In spite of this there would have been some antisocial behaviour. The most notorious perpetrator, however, came from outside the area. Dick Turpin is said to have made travel dangerous in Epping Forest and even to have mugged a gentleman in Nazeing Wood in 1734.

Clearly the churchwardens and overseers would have needed to write and be proficient at simple arithmetic. Due to this level of education they would have had some standing in the village. They would have become well known due to the responsibility they held for ensuring that the rates were paid during their year of office. These posts were almost always held by men but there are records of several women including Mary Acres in 1723, Sarrah Camp (probably from Ninnings) in 1736, and Alice Chandler (possibly from Queens Cottage) in 1741.

Both the churchwardens and overseers set rates to be paid by those in the village who occupied land. The charges were based on the acreage in their occupation. The income from the churchwardens' rates was used to pay costs associated with the Church of England, which would surely have rankled with the nonconformists. It appears that even those loyal to the Church of England had reason to complain because the behaviour of Nazeing's vicars seems to have been rather deleterious. Joseph Browne's replacement appointed as vicar was George Hawdon (or Harding) who, in 1668, was accused of "being a common tippler and one that frequents alehouses very much". That the well loved Browne was forced to resign so that such a person could be appointed would have strengthened the resolve of the nonconformists. Other vicars were noted for their absence. For example George Manley was Nazeing's vicar from 1721 to 1752 but appears not to have been attending the Vestry meetings as he was absent on service as a naval chaplain. In 1721 it was ordered by the Vestry that "the Vicar of the parish shall attend all vestreys on the penalty of 1/-". In 1761 Thomas Salt became the vicar for 44 years. He too is described as being a non-resident for much of this period. The records make frequent mention of assistant curates, who would have been deputising for absent vicars.

By the 1770s, however, the period without local clerical and lay leadership was coming to an end. The arrival in Nazeing of William Palmer, who bought Lucas Hill Farm in 1772, and of James Bury, who moved into Leonards Green Farm in 1797, brought a new approach which caused a change of attitude among the villagers. Soon, of those who had been described as "a sad lawless set", it would be said "now there is not a better set in the country".

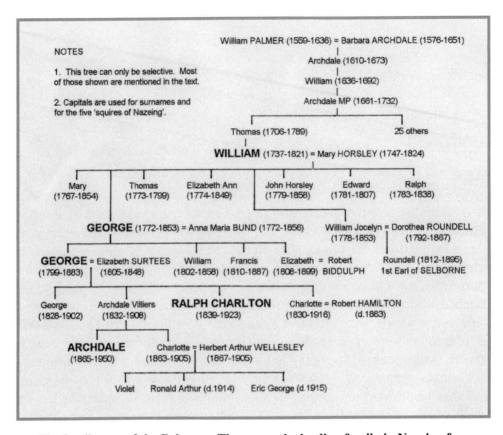

NOTES

1. This tree can only be selective. Most of those shown are mentioned in the text.

2. Capitals are used for surnames and for the five 'squires of Nazeing'.

William PALMER (1559-1636) = Barbara ARCHDALE (1576-1651)

Archdale (1610-1673)

William (1636-1692)

Archdale MP (1661-1732)

Thomas (1706-1789)   25 others

WILLIAM (1737-1821) = Mary HORSLEY (1747-1824)

Mary (1767-1854)   Thomas (1773-1799)   Elizabeth Ann (1774-1849)   John Horsley (1779-1858)   Edward (1781-1807)   Ralph (1783-1838)

GEORGE (1772-1853) = Anna Maria BUND (1772-1856)   William Jocelyn = Dorothea ROUNDELL (1778-1853) (1792-1867)

GEORGE (1799-1883) = Elizabeth SURTEES (1805-1848)   William (1802-1858)   Francis (1810-1887)   Elizabeth (1808-1899) = Robert BIDDULPH   Roundell (1812-1895) 1st Earl of SELBORNE

George (1828-1902)   Archdale Villiers (1832-1908)   **RALPH CHARLTON** (1839-1923)   Charlotte (1830-1916) = Robert HAMILTON (d.1883)

ARCHDALE (1865-1950)   Charlotte (1863-1905) = Herbert Arthur WELLESLEY (1867-1905)

Violet   Ronald Arthur (d.1914)   Eric George (d.1915)

The family tree of the Palmers. They were the leading family in Nazeing for nearly two centuries. Below is a photograph from about 1900 of Nazeing Park, built by William Palmer in about 1795, and owned by the family for more than one hundred years.

CHAPTER 5

"A RESPECTABLE LITTLE VILLAGE"

The rise of the Palmers and the Burys, 1778 to 1851

In 1790 the vicar of Nazeing stated that there were "no families of note" in the parish but in 1810 the curate recorded the presence of "William Palmer Justice of the Peace and James Bury Esquire". By 1847 the Palmer family owned 760 acres, almost one fifth of the parish, and the Burys around 300. Whereas John Johnson, the Rector of Great Parndon, had stated that "the villagers of Nazeing were a sad, lawless set until Mr Palmer took them in hand", in 1831 Thomas Wright described Nazeing as "a respectable little village". Contemporaries saw the presence or absence of resident gentry as crucial to the moral tone of a village. Nazeing farmers and labourers had been used to doing much as they wished but now they knew that at any time their landlord was likely to ride up and check on their activities. The story of Nazeing in this period is therefore best told in terms of the influence of the Palmers and, to a lesser extent, the Burys.

The Palmer family

Early in the seventeenth century William Palmer, the second son of a Staffordshire yeoman, married an heiress named Barbara Archdale and bought an estate at Wanlip in Leicestershire. The family made a substantial fortune through sheep-farming and developed commercial links with London, where they became leading members of the Mercers' Company. William's great-grandson, Archdale, became M.P. for Leicester and produced 26 children, one of whom, Thomas, was the father of William Palmer of Nazeing.

In 1766 William married Mary Horsley. They had six sons, all of whom made their way in the professions, and two unmarried daughters. Their grandson, Roundell Palmer (1812-1895), was a major political figure, who was created Earl of Selborne during Gladstone's first premiership and became Lord Chancellor. As a boy he often visited his Nazeing relatives; his memoirs are a valuable source of information about them. Selborne described his grandparents as "...warm and constant in their friendships, kind and good neighbours, to poor as well as rich; and

William Palmer painted by an unknown artist about the time he built Nazeing Park.

both in the country and in London hospitable and sociable". Surviving letters suggest that it was Mrs Palmer and her daughters who kept an affectionate but scattered family together with lively and intelligent correspondence. The Palmers soon began to move in the circles of the west Essex gentry.

On Christmas Eve 1790 Mrs Palmer wrote to her daughter Elizabeth:

> We are not without our Gaiety here, our friends at Mark Hall are returned & puzzling how to amuse <u>with variety</u> the Neighbourhood. [We were not in the mood and sent our excuses but] ... A note was returned by Mrs Burgoyne to say they would not admit of such a desertion...

This episode would not be out of place in the pages of Jane Austen. The Burgoynes of Mark Hall were leading figures among the west Essex gentry and Mrs Burgoyne's insistence shows that the Palmers had been accepted rapidly. Montagu Burgoyne was the younger brother of General "Gentleman Johnny" Burgoyne, who was defeated by the Americans at Saratoga. He was a keen advocate of agricultural improvement and encouraged the newly revived sport of fox-hunting, which was enjoyed by the Palmer brothers also.

William's eldest son George (1772-1853) was "distinguished by great Integrity ... and a life guided by Religion & Duty". He married Anna Maria Bund, daughter and co-heir of a Worcestershire squire, whose "modest and sweet sensibility would soothe the most troubled spirit". They had four children and George's meticulous character is suggested by his recording, every new year's day, their heights to the nearest quarter-inch.

George learnt the art of navigation with the East India Company which, when he was only sixteen, gave him command of a merchantman. The narrow escape of some of his sailors from drowning led to his life-long interest in safety at sea and a reputation as a philanthropist which earned him a place in the *Dictionary of National Biography*. He continued the Palmer mercantile tradition: as Master of the Mercers' Company he participated in the coronation of George IV and in 1832 he was chairman of the Shipowners' Society. For nearly thirty years he was vice-chairman of the National Lifeboat Institution, which used boats designed by him, and he always ensured that his own ships carried life-saving equipment. From 1836 to 1847 he sat as M.P. for South Essex and overcame strong parliamentary opposition to achieve important legislation on maritime safety.

The building of Nazeing Park

In 1772 William Palmer owned eighteen acres in Nazeing, including one farmhouse, Lucas Hill, and one cottage. By the time of his death in 1821 he owned 284 acres, including a mansion, Nazeing Park, and 35 other properties. He did not achieve this at one blow but steadily, building the estate by acquiring various parcels of land, most of them near Nazeing Park, as they came on the market. Typical was the sad case of the Newman family, who owned present day Pond House. Within a few months both parents and one daughter died, so that the family had to pay three admission fines in a short time. The remaining daughter had the double blow of being bereaved and penniless, forcing her executors to sell up. Details of the growth of the estate may be found in David Pracy's unpublished dissertation, *Palmer of Nazing*. Its most important aspect was the building of Nazeing Park.

Palmer and his family moved into Lucas Hill, which was a substantial "tenement with stables, outhouses, yards, gardens, orchards and appurtenances". It was perhaps rather ramshackle and unsuitable for returning hospitality to gentry such as the Burgoynes, so William Palmer decided to build a mansion more suitable for a gentleman. He sited it next to Lucas Hill in a commanding position, which offered not only a prospect for those inside looking out but also an imposing appearance for those outside looking in.

Thomas Palmer's reply to a letter from his sister Elizabeth in 1795 conveys the excitement of the new project:

> So Nazeing is totally transformed, altered and improved within doors and without, but I think I should know it again notwithstanding the metamorphosis. You may impark and impale as much as you please, you may pull down Mr King's little erections and put up Mr Lewis's great erections, I should know it again despite all the architects in the kingdom: every lump of clay will speak & say, I belong to Nazeing ...

"Mr King" was Robert King, a publican and carpenter by trade, who graduated to surveying and building and did work for the vestry. He produced a map and survey for the Palmers and provided the food and drink at their tenants' annual Christmas party. As an Overseer of the Poor King was a man of some importance in the village but Palmer, when planning his new house, looked further afield. "Mr Lewis" was James Lewis, a noted neo-classical architect, whose best known work was the Bethlehem Hospital for Lunatics (now the Imperial War Museum), but whose best work was probably a series of elegantly restrained country houses similar to Nazeing Park.

"I do think," added Thomas Palmer, "the turning of the road over the common to be a most capital improvement." Some eighteenth century landlords shifted entire villages to develop their estates but William

Palmer contented himself with diverting the main road from Waltham Abbey to Epping and Harlow, which ran past the new mansion. In 1796 the vestry agreed that "Mr Palmer should have liberty to stop up and remove the present old road", so he paid £150 and agreed to make a new road along the line of a track over Nazeing Common, thirteen feet wide and surfaced by gravel.

In a later letter Thomas wrote:

> From your description of the improvements made & to be made I fancy that I have a pretty correct idea of the ensemble of <u>Nazeing Park</u>. That you approve of them is to my mind the best praise...

William Palmer had bought the old road and several cottages adjoining Nazeingwood Common, thus enabling him to create a fine piece of private parkland. Often at this time homely personal house names gave way to grander titles taken from the whole village; Thomas's underlining refers to the name of the new mansion. In making an apparently small change, however, William Palmer was asserting a role in Nazeing that others were not yet ready to accept.

The "pretensions" of William Palmer

William Palmer was a man of enormous energy. Within three years of moving into Nazeing, he had been elected as a trustee of Nazeingwood Common and initiated plans to remedy its decline. Having been established by one private act, it could be reformed only by another. In 1778 Parliament passed

> An Act for Regulating the Stocking of a certain piece of inclosed Pasture Ground called Nazeing Wood, or Nazeing Park, in the Manor and Parish of Nazeing, in the County of Essex, and for keeping the Fences thereof in Repair...

Palmer put his own money into promoting the Act and became treasurer to Nazeing Wood or Park.

For twenty years he worked harmoniously with his four fellow-trustees, but then, between 1797 and 1803, they all died or were not re-elected. New trustees were elected and suddenly Palmer became vulnerable. James Bury of Leonards and John Smith, who occupied Nazeing Lodge and Harold's Park Farm, were new gentry who perhaps saw Palmer as a rival for power. Thomas Banks and William Standingford bought and continued to farm the properties where their forebears had been tenants, and may have resented him as a new arrival changing old ways. Their opportunity to challenge him came in a long-running dispute over common rights.

The 1778 Act had required the trustees to give to the lord of the manor a list of the 98 common right holders, which was copied in the minute book of Nazeing Wood or Park. This number was not sacrosanct at first. In 1784 the trustees built a new pindar's house on the site of a cottage which "hath been suffered to fall down and is now laid waste", and had to trawl the memories of the oldest inhabitants to establish that the cottage had ever existed. Therefore it cannot have appeared on the list. When, however, in 1796 the trustees appointed a new pindar, they had no difficulty in agreeing that "he shall for his encouragement enjoy a commoning". In 1799, with their approval, Palmer entered into the minute book an updated list of houses with common rights, into which he incorporated two additional properties, the pindar's house and a cottage on the site of 42 North Street.

In 1801 James Bury was elected as a trustee and Palmer made his largest single purchase, 77 acres in Lower Nazeing which he bought from Jacob Bosanquet, lord of the manor of Broxbourne. This included Mansion House Farm, Burnt Hall Farm, and five cottages, one of them Palmer's addition to the 1799 list. While Palmer was building up his estate in Upper Nazeing, Bury was doing the same in Lower Nazeing. If, as seems likely, he too wanted to buy these properties, he would have been angered by Palmer's intervention. Certainly over the next few years Bury was a prime mover in a prolonged and malicious attack on Palmer.

Over the years Palmer had made various small but unauthorised alterations to the minute book. At a special meeting on Boxing Day 1808 John Sympson Jessopp, a barrister and rightholder, put forward a motion that

> the number of common rights cannot be increased by any pretensions whatsoever ... it is highly unjustifiable and improper for any Trustee or any other person to alter any Minute of any proceeding in the Book of those interested in this Common...

On the proposal of Jessopp and Bury the next meeting of the rightholders agreed to send the minute book to Palmer so that he could change the unauthorised entries. Not only did he refuse to do so, he also copied into the book two affidavits asserting that the tenant before 1778 had exercised common rights. He walked out of the 1809 Annual General Meeting in protest at the refusal to accept his claim and the next year was not re-

**A page from the minute book of Nazeing Wood or Park for Boxing Day 1808,
recording John Sympson Jessop's attack on the "pretensions" of William Palmer
and the signatures of 17 leading landholders who were present at the meeting.**

elected as a trustee. In 1812 the meeting resolved to delete the
controversial affidavits, although legal opinion supported Palmer on the
grounds that the number of rights was not specified in the Act. The
cottage retained its common right.

The whole episode is a vivid illustration of petty parish politics. At the
1812 meeting Jessopp announced his intention to move a resolution that

the Public Road or Highway from Nazeing to Harlow which formerly passed by the Door of the House of this William Palmer Esq. which was diverted and turned by him of his own great benefit and convenience around this common called Nazeing Park was so diverted and turned without the consent of the Freeholders and Copyholders and without any satisfaction having been made to them.

The actions of Palmer and the language of Bury and Jessopp show considerable malice on both sides although in reviving the issue of the road diverted sixteen years earlier Jessopp was probably expressing a more generally held view. Bury and Jessopp seem to have persuaded the other three trustees to go along with them and, although different individuals were involved, their persistent and costly opposition to Palmer contrasts strikingly with the casual granting of a common right to the pindar's cottage.

The rift was partially healed. Although William Palmer was never again a trustee, in December 1814 he attended a trustees' meeting to discuss the purchase of an East India Bond, a subject for which his mercantile expertise would have been invaluable. On the death of John Smith in 1819 William's son, George, was elected as a trustee.

William Palmer and the poor

In his conversation with the eminent agricultural writer Arthur Young, John Johnson was correct in attributing the transformation of the "sad lawless set" in Nazeing to "Mr Palmer". Young commented that the 1778 Act was a "very extraordinary regulation of a most valuable common" which had previously been

> stocked in a manner that deprived the poor of a benefit which they might, under a better arrangement, have derived from such a fine tract of land...WILLIAM PALMER, Esq., who possesses considerable property here, had the praiseworthy humanity to offer to lay down money to enable every poor man, otherwise unable to find stock, to buy ten sheep, the produce of which was to be his until he was repaid, and then to remain the cottager's.

As well as making these loans, Palmer devised a variety of imaginative schemes of benefit to the people of the village, including himself.

As early as 1693 it was recorded that the vestry ordered pauper children to be "bound apprentice" as they had previously but this arrangement seems to have fallen into disuse, perhaps though lack of money. In 1788, Palmer in conjunction with the vestry, revived the apprenticeship scheme which was designed to "place out Children whose parents or themselves are burthensome to this Parish". Thirty-four ratepayers agreed to "bind themselves to Mr William Palmer in the penal sum of 40s" so that each in turn as determined by lot would accept any child aged eight (later raised to twelve) as an apprentice for five years and "find wholesome food, raiment and lodging". When this period was ended the subscriber would "furnish them with decent cloathing and 40s and Mr William Palmer adding thereunto 20s". If the ratepayer declined the child, he would pay Palmer a 20s forfeit and pass the child on to the next subscriber. No child should go to "anyone thought improper to be trusted", although anyone so disbarred would not pay the 20s forfeit. In 1804 the scheme was reviewed and it was declared that "great benefit has been derived therefrom", so the arrangement was renewed. At the same time it was agreed that "any Inhabitant may at any time select a parish Child as an apprentice ... and be considered as having complied with this obligation".

These schemes established Palmer's right to be considered the unofficial squire of Nazeing and he steadily built on this reputation. In the crisis year of 1795 he paid the 4s land tax contribution for one of his tenants, Widow Sibthorpe, and two years later he organised and financed the digging of a new pond on his own land for the benefit of the commoners. In 1798 the normally rather austere Jocelyn Palmer, third son of William and father of Roundell, told his sister Elizabeth about the celebrations of Nelson's victory at the Battle of the Nile:

> We even made an effort at Nazeing, demolishing a box of my father's
> candles and fumigating the house with tallows, burning a whole stack of
> wood and distributing to Mankind in general I don't know how many gallons
> of ale.

As Napoleon's continental blockade and increasing demand for food meant that men of substance throughout Essex were constantly seeking ways of improving production, the Palmers and Burys were typical in trying various agricultural experiments. The quarrel between William Palmer and James Bury reached almost absurd proportions when, in an attempt to improve the quality of the sheep on the Common, Palmer offered to provide Southdown rams and Bury countered with an offer of Leicesters. The matter went to a vote which Palmer won 17-10. Voting under the 1778 Nazeing Wood or Nazeing Park Act was in accordance with the number of common rights held, so it is likely that most of the votes on both sides were cast by Palmer and Bury themselves.

In 1802, after another two years of scarcity, Palmer provided a post-mill "on a plan of selling Flour to the Poor ... under the shop price and for the general convenience of the neighbourhood". Strategically located on a high piece of Palmer's own ground just off Betts Lane, it was built by the noted Essex millwright James Turtle at a cost of £576 4s 5d. The mill measured 19 by 11 feet and housed two pairs of French stones. In 1805 a building with a house and store, measuring 50 by 20 feet, was added at a cost of £250. In its first two full years the mill made a healthy net profit of about twenty per cent per annum.

The mill demonstrates Palmer's ability to combine good works with the making of a useful profit but his activities probably had another motive as well. The year of his arrival in Nazeing had seen, for the first time, Essex agricultural labourers join townspeople in food riots which, though they were soon suppressed, made a profound impact on the ruling elite. Palmer's mercantile connections would have alerted him to revolutionary movements in the newly independent United States and elsewhere, so he began making his loans twenty years before such schemes became commonplace in Essex. Like most squires he was a staunch Tory, who was horrified by the French Revolution, and his wife deplored the "shocking and brutal trial of Queen Marie Antoinette". Palmer built or extended at least ten cottages, mainly to accommodate the additional labour needed on his estate but perhaps also, like his neighbour John Conyers of Copped Hall, who undertook a similar programme, to help tame the "outcasts" of Epping Forest.

The Palmers, like many gentry, saw education as a way of averting unrest and in the early 1790s established a School of Industry, one of over twenty in Essex, which were intended to teach children practical skills and religious obedience. They worked in conjunction with the Society for the Promotion of Industry in the Hundreds of Harlow and Ongar and the Half-Hundred of Waltham which, in 1797, awarded prizes for flax-spinning and needlework to seven Nazeing children. In 1796-7 Palmer acquired from the vestry the old poorhouse on Church Green and in exchange gave them the School of Industry building which became the new poorhouse. At the manorial court on 30th May 1798 "William Palmer Esq., William Welch and John Banks ... three of the Principal Inhabitants of this parish" were admitted tenants of the poorhouse, which they were "to hold ... upon trust for the benefit of the Poor Inhabitants of the parish of Nazeing". Palmer therefore replaced the School of Industry with a new school, which in 1803 was being attended by 37 children and in 1810 was described by curate Foster as "Miss Palmer's school". The

Church of England was waking from its long slumber and a new Society for Educating the Poor in the Principles of the Established Church was encouraging the development of schools in rural areas. The Palmers, as devout Anglicans, supported this initiative. By 1828 their school had become a National School with fifty pupils.

The growth of the Palmer estate

If William Palmer's major achievement was the building of Nazeing Park mansion, George's was the extension and consolidation of the estate. Although on the death of his father George Palmer owned 335 acres in Nazeing, he was not the leading landowner: the Essex historian Elizabeth Ogborne had noted in 1814 that "the lands are, chiefly in this parish, the property of Joseph Bird, esq." Bird was a substantial property owner who lived at Upton in Essex. In 1822 Palmer paid him £4680 for the 170 acre Nazeing Lodge Farm, which was described in the sale particulars as "so near the *Town of Epping* that the butter made on this Farm is celebrated for its goodness, in the London Market, as some of the finest under the name of EPPING BUTTER." Lodge Farm was George Palmer's largest purchase and its sale marked a major shift in the balance of landholding in Nazeing. By 1824 he had 529 acres, James Bury 336, and Bird 176, although the lord of the manor, Sir William Wake, was still comfortably the leading owner, with 785.

Like his father, George acquired one of his properties in tragic circumstances. Belchers Farm had been in the Knight and Lucas families since 1666; in 1830 it was inherited by William Lucas's only surviving daughter, Laura. She married a Londoner called Charles Deacon but shortly afterwards she and her infant daughter died. He, lacking the same attachment to the farm, sold it to Palmer for £1995.

In 1838 the vestry needed to raise money for its contribution to the new Epping Poor Law Union's workhouse and so it obtained approval from Edwin Chadwick, Secretary to the Poor Law Commissioners, to sell two properties which it owned. The auction details show that there is nothing new in the twentieth century estate agent's penchant for emphasising the good points of an older house and glossing over any costs of improving it. The first property, situated in "a neighbourhood most respectable", was the old poorhouse, "a brick copyhold tenement...built forty years ago by Mr Palmer the principal landed Proprietor upon the Waste for the benefit of the Parish..." It "contained

Vine, Heather, and Clematis Cottages, Betts Lane from a photograph of around 1900. The building was first the School of Industry and then the parish poorhouse, before it was purchased by George Palmer in 1838 and converted into three dwellings.

eleven large rooms with two staircases which at a trifling expense may be turned into four good houses". The second was an almshouse, described as "four freehold tenements pleasantly situated on the side of the Common ... a short distance from Nazeing Gate, which will let (after an inconsiderable outlay in repairs) at about £20 p.a." The vestry duly put the properties up for auction at the King Harold's Head and George Palmer bought both, thus acquiring the former School of Industry which his father had exchanged for a property backing on to Nazeing Park. In fact George turned the poorhouse into three dwellings (now Clematis, Heather, and Vine Cottages) and, finding the outlay in repairs far from inconsiderable, pulled down the almshouse. Its remains were still remembered by older residents in the 1920s. It gave its name to the pond which, until recently, lay on the opposite side of Common Road, just south of the junction with Back Lane.

In 25 years the Palmer estate more than doubled in size: by 1847 the family owned 257 plots with a total of 773 acres and held 43 of the 101 common rights. This gave them great social influence in the village, though the estate was not an economic investment. Capital expenditure on the mansion and the estate was at least £40,000 and there were ongoing expenses such as staff wages and repairs to cottages. The overall return on the land was less than three per cent and the Palmers could have made four per cent easily by lending money on the London stock market. So the estate scarcely broke even and had to be subsidised by the family's business interests.

George Palmer in Nazeing society

From around 1793 George Palmer helped his father with the management of the estate and his work in the village; he kept a day-book which is an extraordinary miscellany indicating how varied his activities were. Some Tory paternalists took a stance of supporting the poorer people against heartless employers, mean parish overseers and grasping middlemen, but Palmer, himself a merchant, worked with the parish authorities to control the village with a judicious blend of carrot and stick.

Nazeing, as a forest village, had enjoyed a good supply of wood and charcoal but during the eighteenth century both became much scarcer. In the 1690s three men were presented for lopping trees on the common but a hundred years later the trustees were experimenting with planting trees to provide shade for the animals. The Palmers, and perhaps other landlords, were busy buying up small pieces of waste which could have supplied fuel. Nazeing Grove, a commercial woodland between Nazeing church and the Black Swan, was a source of wood and charcoal until the mid-1790s, when it was cut down and converted to arable fields, probably to help provide timber and food for the war against France.

Earlier in the century, therefore, one manifestation of the general lawlessness in Nazeing had been theft of fuel, which probably went largely unchecked. George Palmer, however, worked closely with the Overseers of the Poor in a scheme, part charity, part deterrent, to sell cheap coal to the villagers. The coal may well have come by sea from north-east England, where Palmer had commercial links. Certainly it was brought by barge up the newly improved Lee Navigation and was unloaded at Broxbourne Bridge. The coal was taken round the village on carts by men such as Robert King, who was paid 14s, although "Mr Welch gave one turn with his waggon gratis". Evidently Palmer made the initial outlay and then recouped some of the money, because he noted that the coals were sold for him by Wilshire the miller; he listed recipients, amounts paid, and names of "those who did not apply". In 1811 he recorded proudly that he had paid 5s 5d per sack, whereas the price at Waltham was 6s. The young squire did not forget his merchant instincts.

In 1815 George Palmer recorded his attempts to improve the intractable clay soil, so vividly described by his brother Thomas:

> Blackstones for bringing Manure a Barge Load 40 tons = 22 or 23 team loads delivered at Broxbourne Bridge from London for 7 gns but not to load or unload. Query would not chalk be a good manure for Meadow.

Probably he pursued the latter idea because the use of chalk on clay was common practice; a few years later James Bury did bring it to Leonards by barge via Ware. In 1817 George planted five acres of mangel-wurzels to feed his pigs but perhaps he was too successful, because they ate only 4½ tons and the crop of 71 tons 2 cwt 36 lb "completely filled the house".

The big house was always a major source of employment in a village and most of it would have been local. George Palmer employed a bailiff, a butler, a cook, a head gardener and his assistants, a dairywoman, footmen, a lady's maid, and other servants, all of whom would normally have received regular remuneration in cash and/or kind. No systematic records survive, although George notes that in the year beginning 30th June 1813 he paid

Maids' wages	617 16 2
Coachman, footman, underfootman, wages and liveries	90 0 0
Groom	52 0 0
Gardiner [sic] wages and seeds	120 0 0

The figure for maids implies that either they were exceptionally well paid or there were at least thirty of them, which would seem excessive for a modest country house; its preciseness suggests accuracy but there is no way of checking what exactly it includes.

George Palmer's day-book also records various individual transactions, which give a random but useful insight into the kinds of jobs that needed doing around the estate and the casual employment opportunities which they provided. The building of Nazeing Park required drains, water closets, pipes, stopcocks, an engine-house, and a 310 gallon cistern which, when full, "served the house 24 days and more ... from 10 to 15 minutes per day". He had a well dug too, at a cost of £79 11s which went mainly on 144 man-days work by "White and 6 labourers". Their rate of pay increased the further they went down, from 4s for each of the first 50 feet to 7s for the last 44, beyond which they could not dig because the clay became mixed with sand. In 1811

Harknett and Adams, both Nazeing men, provided estimates for thatching and tiles respectively. In 1815 Palmer paid £4 5s to have "the fronts of four cottages painted twice over" and received an estimate of £26 for building a bridge over the brook.

New gentry often invented a tradition of hospitality. In 1811 George Palmer instituted an annual Christmas dinner at which "The Company invited are all Cottagers or small Landed Tenants with those who work with Mr Palmer at the Parish". Each year there is a list of the thirty or so who attended, including the occasional woman, though apparently in her capacity as the wife, "girl", or daughter of one of the men, rather than in her own right. The few who did not accept the invitation are noted, with the implication that Palmer disapproved unless the man was genuinely ill, in which case a bowl of broth was sent round to his wife the next day. There are detailed accounts of the costs, which were usually just under £5: the main components were a leg of sirloin beef and at least ten gallons of beer, probably produced on the estate.

Sometimes paternalistic landlords had to exercise discipline rather than generosity. They were always reluctant to dismiss tenants, because it was difficult to obtain good replacements, but if a poor tenant was seen to get away with too much, the landlord could lose respect. In 1817 George told six of the tenants: "Take notice you are to quit all the premises you hold of me in Nazeing at Michaelmas next." There is no indication of what this was about, although 1816 was a difficult year and they may simply have fallen too far in arrears with rent.

In 1827 the trustees of Nazeing Wood or Park accepted an offer from the vestry for the unemployed poor to work on the common, provided that the trustees of whom George Palmer was one, paid two fifths of the costs and Mr Palmer himself paid one fifth. Over the next nine years the trustees paid the Overseers of the Poor a total of £51 12s 9d, so presumably Palmer contributed about £26. The scheme probably ended as a result of the 1834 Poor Law Act, whereby Nazeing became part of the Epping Union.

"Wake Bt. v Palmer M.P."

When George Palmer was elected to the prestigious role of M.P. for South Essex in 1836, Sir William Wake had been the lord of the manor for fifty years. It seems likely that already he was less than happy about the rise of the Palmers. Only a few very insignificant pieces of land passed directly from him to them and there is no record in the papers of either family that the sale of the lordship of the manor to them, as often happened in such circumstances, was even considered. Then in 1838 a court-case brought Wake and Palmer into direct conflict.

Dinah Standingford was daughter-in-law to the trustee of Nazeing Wood or Park who had been in dispute with William Palmer thirty years earlier. It was not unusual for a resourceful widow to take on the management of her late husband's farm and Dinah did so when William Standingford junior died in 1833. Managing over 150 acres, some for Wake and some of her own, she was one of the most substantial farmers in the village. On 25th April 1838 she attempted to cart dung from Hoe Lane to Wake's fields at Nazeing Grove, across the land of Palmer, who instructed his men to block the way with planks and a ditch. It was she who sued him but his solicitor, Joseph Jessopp, emphasised that, though she was the nominal plaintiff, the case was "commenced by Sir William Wake and conducted by his solicitor". On his rough notes Jessopp summarised the dispute between Nazeing's two leading landowners neatly as "Wake Bt. v Palmer M.P.". The plaintiffs argued that their route was "a way of necessity" but George Palmer's brother William, a

The scene of the episode when George Palmer instructed his men to stop Dinah Standingford carting dung from Hoe Lane to Nazeing Grove, thus provoking the Standingford v. Palmer court case.

conveyancer and author of sufficient distinction to appear in *The Dictionary of National Biography*, replied that there were alternative routes, so it was "a self-created necessity".

Therefore the case, which turned upon local precedent, provides information about Nazeing daily life that would otherwise have been lost. This comes from the evidence of various witnesses including the following. William Rand had been employed by William Palmer to take faggots from Nazeing Grove for use on the new road over the common back in 1796. Joseph Wilshire came to Nazeing in 1807 to rent William's newly erected mill and later rented fields from George. Another witness was James Horn, who was William's groom until the latter's death in 1821 but then became a farmer. Lastly there was James Hoad, a carpenter, who was "first employed by William Palmer to look around the fields and fences and report once a year". Given the landowner's influence in any village, it is unsurprising that all four gave evidence for Palmer. One sympathises therefore with Thomas Starling: his landlord was George but his employer was Dinah, and after he had supported her by stating that he had driven along the disputed track, Thomas Ricketts commented that both horse and cart must have jumped a hedge to do it. It indicates George Palmer's fairness as a landlord that Starling was still his tenant in 1841.

The case went to the Chelmsford assizes initially but it was referred for arbitration to Thomas Staples, barrister-at-law, and heard at the King Harold's Head. Appearing for George was Roundell Palmer, newly qualified as a barrister, although cousinly affection did not prevent his doubling the fee from a suggested five guineas to ten. The case was heard soon after the episode which provoked it but, for some reason, it took Staples six months to publish his conclusion. Although most of the witness evidence supported Palmer, Staples found in favour of Dinah Standingford and ordered that Palmer should pay her forty shillings damages.

Over the next 25 years there were several more confrontations between the Wakes and the Palmers but none is recorded between George and Dinah. By 1851 her son William had become his tenant at Mansion House Farm. George died in 1853, Dinah in 1868, and now they both lie in All Saints' churchyard, separated by little more than the length of a horse and cart. It may be that as memories faded the Palmers got their way after all, because the alternative routes described by witnesses are still public footpaths today, whereas Dinah's is shown on the Definitive Map as a private path.

The Burys

If the Palmers were Nazeing's first family, the Burys were its second. There was perhaps a tacit understanding whereby the Palmers exercised influence over the Upper Town and the Common, while the Burys managed the Lower Town.

According to the Bury family records they were associated with Nazeing from 1769. Their settlement in Essex was much earlier than that, however, for the Nazeing branch of the family was descended from the Burys of Bulphan, where they had been for many generations.

The ancestor who founded the family fortunes in Nazeing was the son of an ensign who had fought in India and, "as was so frequent in those days, had found soldiering a not altogether unprofitable occupation." He purchased property in Nazeing but did not live in the parish.

His son, James, was given a house in Nazeing by his father in about 1797 and came there to live when he married. This house was known as Leonards Green House. James Bury engaged in financial transactions in the City of London in which he was closely associated with Messrs. Prescott and Grote, the banking partners who were the founders of the banking firm of Prescott. The Mr. Grote of those days was the historian of Greece and was for many years the trustee of his friend James Bury's Essex property.

In the early 1800s James Bury, just like William Palmer a decade earlier, built a new house, gave it a new name, and diverted a road round it. He prospered and acquired more land in Nazeing and, at his death in 1825, owned a considerable estate which remained in the possession of his descendants for well over a century.

There were many remarkable parallels between the Palmer and Bury families. As a result of the occupational hazards of their class, both families lost sons who were in the prime of life and were deeply touched by these losses. Thomas Palmer and Edmund Bury were both servants of the East India Company and died of illnesses contracted in India, Thomas aged 26 in 1799, Edmund aged 28 in 1824. Edward Palmer was a Royal Navy post-captain, who died in 1807, also aged 26, as the result of a shipwreck; Captain Horatio Bury "was killed at the head of his troop whilst charging the enemy on the 28th August 1842 at the battle of Obah, near Ghuynee in Afghanistan, aged 36".

Both William Palmer and James Bury were elected by the vestry to the unpopular post of Surveyor of Roads, perhaps a neat commentary on their activities in this respect. Often they worked together, for instance, in law enforcement. Yet there was also a degree of rivalry between the two families. The Burys arrived in Nazeing rather later than the Palmers and never owned quite as much land. In 1824, for example, James Bury had 336 acres but George Palmer had 529. The Burys' pedigree, as listed in Burke's *Landed Gentry,* began only with James in 1798, whereas that of the Palmers dated back to 1624 and included M.P.s and baronets. Perhaps this is why sometimes the Burys took the opportunity to score off the Palmers, as with the personal animosity between William Palmer and James Bury in the conflict over the disputed common rights.

The churches

The Palmers and Burys were devout Anglicans, whose memorials are to be seen in All Saints' church. The lay rectory, however, remained with the Wakes and the vicars continued to be appointed by the Lord Chancellor, as they are still. The alliance between gentry and clergy was therefore not necessarily as close as in parishes where the squire could appoint and even force out the parson. Nevertheless they often worked together.

For most of the eighteenth century Nazeing followed the typical Essex pattern of absentee incumbents and ecclesiastical torpor. The tradition continued with Thomas Salt, who was vicar from 1761 to 1805. In 1779 five new bells were installed by Pack and Chapman of Whitechapel. In addition to the name of the makers one of the original five bells bears the names of John Pegrum, who lived at Park Cottages, and of John Walker, who lived at Darmers. Pegrum and Walker were the churchwardens at that time but it is not known whether they contributed towards the cost of the bells. One may suspect the influence of the newly-arrived William Palmer in this initiative.

Four years later Salt was obliged to mortgage the revenues of the vicarage for £198 in order to repair it. In 1790 he told the bishop that "infirmities and the better support of my family are reasons why I am much absent", although he installed his son as curate and "performed residence in my parish September to the last week in October".

By 1797 Salt's curate was Robert Auber, a conscientious clergyman who gave Arthur Young the detailed statistics which he used for his *General View of the Agriculture of Essex*. With the ubiquitous William Palmer, Auber organised a scheme whereby potatoes for distribution to the poor were grown on "the parish ground" (probably the field where Bumbles Green Leisure Centre is now situated). Palmer and Auber directed the annual planting and digging of the potatoes and the hoeing and weeding of the land by the poor themselves, who were "to have ½ a peck for every bushel as an encouragement for doing their Duty". The scheme was still operating in 1825.

Salt was succeeded by John Moir who, in 1810, was employing John Foster as curate at a salary of £50 per annum. Foster told the bishop that Moir "had been at Ramsgate for the benefit of his health for eight months past". Perhaps that was an excusable absence because Moir's two sons died in 1810 and 1811 and Moir himself died in 1812. Foster added that services were held on alternate Sundays and that the sacraments were administered four times a year to thirty or forty communicants, with

Nazeings' vicarage until 1956 when a new one was built. It is now two residences called the Old Vicarage and the Glebe House. From a postcard of about 1910.

collections being "disposed to the Poor".

Over the next 25 years Nazeing's vicars were, on the whole, more notable for their activities outside the parish than in it. Charles Arnold (1813-1818) lived in Nazeing but was also vicar of Roydon and held services alternately in the two parishes. In 1818 he resigned his post and was baptised at Potter Street Baptist Church. George Pellew (1819-1821) was the son of Viscount Exmouth and married the daughter of the former Prime Minister, Henry Addington, whose biography he wrote. His short incumbency, during which he employed two curates, was probably little more than a staging post for his later jobs as Canon of Canterbury and Dean of Norwich. Little is known of Henry Fuedall (1821-1828) but Charles Dyson (1828-1834) was described as "an admirable priest and a man of deep learning". At the age of only 24 he had been appointed Professor of Anglo-Saxon at Oxford University, but he resigned to take up holy orders. For three years he employed Arthur Hubbard as curate at a salary of £120 per year, which was notably more generous than that offered by John Moir twenty years earlier.

During the eighteenth century the spiritual poverty of the Church of England did little to cater for followers of the Puritan tradition, which did not disappear entirely but went underground. When therefore, in 1792, the Countess of Huntingdon's Connexion, an evangelical sect, moved its training college for ministers to Cheshunt and began to evangelize the surrounding area, it met with a ready response. The powerful preaching of John James, a young student whose first pulpit was reported to be a "venerable tree" near the pound at the crossroads by Nazeing Bury, led to the formation of a congregation in Nazeing. In 1797 the house of James Ford, probably on the site of Shiree in St. Leonards Road, was licensed for independent worship, which took place in

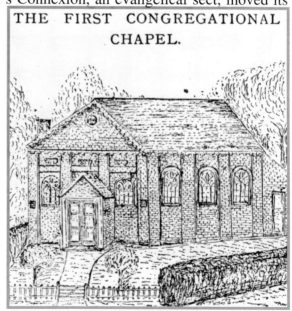

THE FIRST CONGREGATIONAL CHAPEL.

The original Congregational Chapel, built in 1816.

a "lowly shed" with Isaac Nicholson, principal of the college, as the minister. The congregation flourished so that by 1816 the shed had proved too small. A new chapel was built by Charles Hollingsworth in Middle Street, on a piece of freehold land which he sold to the trustees of Cheshunt College. It was paid for with subscriptions from the congregation and a generous donation by the trustees, in whom the deeds were vested.

Though the chapel continued to have close links with the college, gradually it developed a sturdy life of its own. Paradoxically the chapel probably benefited from the more law-abiding atmosphere created by the Anglican Palmers and Burys, although as late as 1821 a report written for the college noted that "the congregation at Nazeing is beyond expectation considering the malevolent influence exerted to prevent persons from attending to the gospel". This tantalisingly vague sentence probably refers to the remnants of the "sad lawless set" but it was perhaps this very opposition that encouraged the congregation to form themselves into a separate "society", which included several members with some influence in the village. William Collins farmed 300 acres at Nazeing Bury for Sir William Wake. Samuel and Elizabeth Pegrum at Greenleaves, Samuel's brother William at Darmers, John Nicholls at Camps, and James Matthews at Belchers all managed substantial farms for absentee landlords. George and Elizabeth Standingford of Mansion House Farm and Joseph Wilshire the miller were both tenants of George Palmer, which suggests that he did not oppose the new venture.

The villagers

Although for much of the country the period between the American Revolution and the Great Exhibition of 1851 was one of economic dislocation and social unrest, Nazeing escaped the worst of this. The population grew by an average of four persons a year, from fewer than 600 in 1778 to a peak of 824 in 1841, after which it settled at around 770 for the rest of the century.

Arthur Young calculated that between 1778 and 1800 Nazeing had a net population increase of 84, whereas in neighbouring Great Parndon, which was less well managed, the population actually went down. He attributed this to the regulation of the common and William Palmer's loan scheme, which recognised that the poorer people could not afford to invest money in sheep and cattle to put on the common. Many accepted loans and all repaid them from the profits within two years or less. Young's suggestion that rises in poor rates, although considerable, might have been far worse without the loans is borne out because, by the end of the war in 1815, they were significantly lower in Nazeing than in comparable west Essex parishes.

In 1778 four common right cottages were unoccupied but soon landowners such as William Palmer, James Bury, and Barnard Acres were active in building to house the increasing numbers of people. Young's description of typical Essex cottages suggests what they may have been like:

> Modern built cottages...are very superior to the old ones, being erected with brick and covered with tile...but the old cottages are generally of clay daubing, in bad repair, and very imperfectly covered with thatch. New cottages in the larger part of the county are much wanted, as appears sufficiently evident in the high price of labour...

Paradoxically, war-time conditions contributed to the boom time. A combination of high demand and, after 1802, good harvests meant that demand for food was high, prices were good, and Nazeing prospered. Even though rents almost doubled, farmers such as Thomas Banks and William Standingford were able to buy the properties of which they had been tenants. Their new status was recognised in their election to important offices in the vestry and on the common.

Although strongly influenced by William Palmer, the vestry continued as an independent body, conscientiously making provision for the needs of the poorer people. When appropriate, they paid for nursing, lodgings, faggots (for fuel), tools, and clothes including shoes, shirts, gowns, stays, breeches, and a smock-frock. They paid for "Docters Stuf" also and, when that was unavailing, for funeral expenses.

Typical was the case of Edward Biat, for whom in 1784 the vestry bought a spade, a mattock, and an axe. Presumably this was so that he could work as an agricultural labourer and not be a charge on them, in which case the policy was successful, because for the next ten years there is no mention of him in the vestry minutes. Then evidently he was taken mortally ill and there is a sad record of his final days:

Edw Biat & family	1 17 0
Bottle of wine for Biat	2 6
Mary Matthis for sitting up with him	7 0
For laying him out	1 0
Bureing [sic] fees	5 0

> For the coffeedary   1 0
> Coffin, sroud [sic], beer & bread & cheese   16 0

Obviously "the coffeedary" was related to the funeral. It is not a word known to the compilers of the *Oxford English Dictionary* but they suggest that it may represent the term "co-feudary", a fee payable on the death of a manorial tenant.

Overseers of the Poor had always been elected annually but in 1803 it was reported that "the Parishoners do further agree to Nominate Abraham Pegrum Jun.r for a Perpettual Overseer at the Sallery of £10.0.0 A Year Ten parishonare Agreeing to the above and four parishoner only Disagreeing". At this time Abraham Pegrum Junior (1771 to *c.*1829) was the occupant of Darmers and farmed with his father at Greenleaves about eighty acres of land.

The manorial courts continued their slow decline but were still of some importance as the forum for dealing with property transactions and agricultural misdemeanours. In 1803, for example, William Welch suffered the indignity of being presented, at a court held in his own house. He had used the commons which, as tenant of Nazeing Bury, he was not entitled to do.

As often happens, peacetime brought economic slump and social hardship, especially for the poorer people. Parliament, still chiefly representing landed interests, passed the Corn Laws, which decreed that foreign wheat should be imported only when home prices reached 80s a quarter. Food prices increased steeply and riots were particularly serious in East Anglia. They were avoided in Nazeing, perhaps only with a judicious retreat by the Trustees of Nazeing Wood or Park. Common rights could mean the difference between survival and starvation. Already in 1790 the trustees had aroused some resentment by ordering that the common should be cleared of stock for six weeks so that the grass could renew itself. In 1807 this period was extended to the whole of January and February but, probably because it was a comparatively prosperous time, there was no recorded opposition. However, the trustees provoked outright rebellion when, at the AGM of 1816, they resolved on a further extension to 25th March. The winter was exceptionally harsh and on 19th February 1817 they were forced to call a special meeting at which they had

> laid before them a request from a very large number of persons ... stating that such order would be very hurtful to all the poorer persons exercising right of common as they have nowhere to put their stock till so late a period

as the 25 March next and also taking into account the present distressing time.

The trustees made a temporary concession and admitted stock on 1st March 1817 but then went to the trouble and expense of seeking a legal opinion. In their evidence the trustees asserted that because the order was

> inconvenient to several persons turning Stock on the Common and who have no Land of their own ... [those persons] have been round the Parish obtaining from Cottagers and others who have no right of Common a requisition against such order.

A long and convoluted opinion theoretically supported them on the grounds that their decision was a legitimate means of managing the common and they could be put out at the AGM. Then they resolved that stock should be admitted on 1st March 1818 after all, a significant victory for the poorer cottagers.

Law and order

The gentry of Nazeing played an important part in suppressing crime and unrest in west Essex, particularly before the establishment of the Essex Constabulary in 1839. William Palmer and James Bury, together with James Pattison of Epping, were trustees of the Association for the Security of the Lives and Properties of the Inhabitants of the Epping Division and the Parts Adjacent. In January 1818 Palmer, now over eighty years old but as combative as ever, published a list of felonies committed in the district. Pattison was the most notable sufferer and had the greatest variety of items stolen. In Nazeing the preferred target was sheep and the victims were mostly farmers and craftsmen. James Wilshire, for example, as well as losing some potatoes, was the only person on the list to be assaulted, not an uncommon fate for a miller. In 1823 thieves broke in and stole saplings and cabbages from the land of Bury, who offered a reward of two pounds.

Agricultural unrest in England culminated in 1830, when revolution in Europe and a second successive poor harvest at home led to an outbreak of arson, wage riots, and breaking of threshing machines, often marked by threatening letters sent in the name of the fictitious Captain Swing. The disturbances swept through most of the low paid corn growing areas of south and east England but Hertfordshire and west Essex were little affected. They came no closer to Nazeing than Sheering and Bishop's Stortford. This was probably because its mixed agriculture

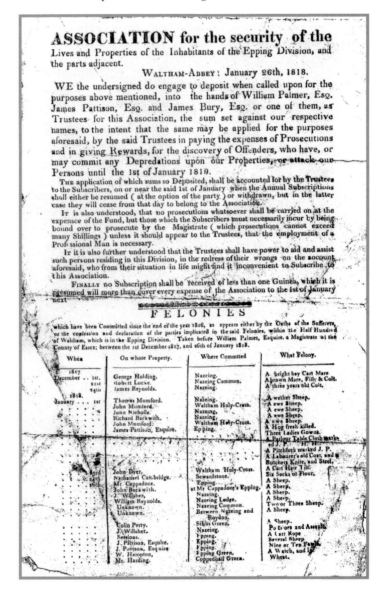

The end of the Napoleonic wars resulted in great economic and social dislocation, so William Palmer and James Bury sank their differences to become leading figures in an association that vigorously fought the consequent increase in crime.

made it less dependent on the grain harvest and its being near London meant relatively high wages and a ready market for its meat and hay.

Nazeing's immunity would also have owed much to the presence of the Palmers and Burys. In December 1830 George Palmer junior raised the West Essex Yeomanry Cavalry for the protection of life and property. The government was concerned to defend the Waltham Abbey powder mills and the Enfield small arms factory, so Palmer's initiative was encouraged by Lord Melbourne and the Duke of Wellington. In April 1831, when a "riotous mob" set fire to some haystacks near the powder mills and rekindled the flames two or three times, the Yeomanry extinguished the fires and restored order. When in 1834 the harsh new Poor Law was introduced, there were fresh riots in the eastern counties and the Bishop's Stortford workhouse was set on fire. There is, however, no record of any major protests in the Epping Union, of which Nazeing was a part; it is likely that some Nazeing men belonged to the Yeomanry. At the time of the Chartist demonstrations in 1848 the Yeomanry again stood by to defend Waltham Abbey and Enfield against potential threats again but this time nothing happened. As the middle of the century approached, Nazeing was in a moderately settled and prosperous state.

An officer of the West Essex Yeomanry Cavalry 1846.

121

Two of Nazeing's public houses. Above is The Red Lion photographed about 1910 following its rebuilding in 1888. This is now the White House in Middle Street. Below is The Crown by the River Lea from a 1907 postcard. Both were already public houses in the 1840s.

CHAPTER 6

MID 19th CENTURY NAZEING - A PROFILE

Despite its proximity to London and the opening, in 1842, of the London to Cambridge railway with stations at Waltham Cross and Broxbourne, mid nineteenth century Nazeing was still a remote rural community. In his *History of Essex*, published in 1831, Thomas Wright described the village's general situation as pleasant and healthy. Most people lived and worked within the parish boundary. In the 1850s farm and common land, much of it arable, made up the village with the principal roads following much the same routes as today. However surfaces were poor and in some places were impassable when flooding occurred. Houses and cottages were timber-framed or brick and were spread through the parish, mostly on sites occupied since the fourteenth century. All Saints' church had been little changed for four hundred years. On Middle Street, however, there stood the original Congregational church, made of wood with a brick front, and on Betts Lane there was a windmill, fully operational.

The number of people living in Nazeing in 1851 was 756 (411 males, 345 females). Most people had been born in the vicinity, 474 in Nazeing, 62 in Roydon, Waltham Abbey or Epping, 68 from elsewhere in Essex, 57 in Hertfordshire leaving only ten per cent from other English counties and London. Of the family names still found in the village, a hundred and fifty years on, there were in the 1851 census returns 23 Mansfields, 22 Nicholls, 18 Pegrums (Pigram), 15 Kings, 11 Starlings and 8 Judds. Standingford was a very common name but is no longer registered here today. There are still descendants of the Coleman, Hale, and Harknett families.

The economy

In 1847, when the Tithe Award Map and Apportionment was drawn up, the parish covered 3957 acres, of which 691 acres of land were free from payment of tithes. The 3266 acres which were tithed consisted of 656 acres of arable land, 1738 meadow or pasture, 37 woodland, 78 homesteads, 633 commons, and 124 roads and water. In October of that year £486 was raised in tithes. The money was divided, £251 going to Sir Charles Wake Baronet, of Courteen Hall in the County of

Northamptonshire, lord of the manor of Nazeing and £235 to the vicar, the Reverend Elisha Hood. Together with a house and 22 acres of glebe land this was his annual living, sufficient to keep two servants.

The tithe map gives a detailed picture of the ownership and the use of land in Nazeing. It shows the field names, some of which have passed in recent years to residential roads, such as Banes Down, Hyde Mead, Pound [Close], Tatsfield [Avenue], Langfield [Close], North Barn, and Great Meadow.

There were at that time sixty-five landowners, nine of whom owned more than a hundred acres each. The two largest were Sir Charles Wake (786 acres) and George Palmer (639 acres). The largest tenant farmers were Edward Collins at Nazeing Bury (299 acres), George Palmer (260) almost all owned by him including Nazeing Lodge and Nazeing Park, John Gray at Langridge (215), William Shepherd Bury (212) all owned by his family including most of Saint Leonards, Saint Lawrence and Snowes, Dinah Standingford (184) including her own White House Farm, William Desforges at Harold's Park (176), George Banks (174) including his own Paynes, Elizabeth Pegrum (145) including Greenleaves, John Nicholls (118) including Camps which he owned and Belchers, and William Pegrum (104) including Darmers.

The economy remained primarily agricultural. Most people who did not obtain their living directly from the land were in associated trades. By 1851 there were twenty-three farmers in the village, thirty-four farmers' families, and 190 farm workers. Supporting them were eight haybinders and carters, four blacksmiths, three wheelwrights, a 'rat ketcher', and the miller and his labourer at the windmill. A carrier to London left the house of George Cater on Tuesdays, returning the following day. George Fairchild, postmaster and shopkeeper, dispatched outgoing post at 6.00p.m. Incoming letters went first to Waltham Abbey, then by footpost, arriving in Nazeing at 9.30a.m.

The largest category of employment after farming was domestic service for the gentlemen and landowners. At Nazeing Park the Palmer family maintained a butler, a footman, a cook and housekeeper, two lady's maids, a kitchen maid, two housemaids, a laundress, and a manservant. At the other end of the scale twenty-one people, including a Chelsea Pensioner, received poor relief.

A rare photograph of All Saints before its spire was removed in 1899.

The churches

By the middle of the nineteenth century the Congregational church was beginning to attract a good number of followers. Average attendance on Sunday was between fifty and sixty and a lean-to addition at the back of the chapel housed a Sunday school. Two services on Sunday were taken by students from Cheshunt College, who probably walked to Nazeing. Joshua Pegrum recalled the old chapel in his memoirs:

> A little vestry just inside the door. The menfolk would sit on the left hand side of the central aisle, the women in the right, except a few family pews in the front where we sat. I can well remember the marks under the women's seats made by the marks of their wooden clogs when they came in wet and dirty. Also holes in the rail in front of where we sat, to hold the tallow candles, the only possible light in those days.

As the church flourished and attendance increased, the brick and wood building was replaced by the present one.

At All Saints', the Reverend Elisha Hood served as Vicar for thirty years spanning the middle of the century. Although he was one of the longest serving vicars and spent more time in the parish than his predecessors, there is little written evidence about the time he lived in Nazeing or what went on within the church. Apparently the plaster chancel arch was installed during his tenure but conditions inside the building were poor. Seating of rough oak with grotesque carved ends was 300 years old. Wright had noted that the parsonage house was a good old building, near the church, moated round.

The account of income produced in 1834 by the Reverend Elisha Hood to support an application for a mortgage to improve the Vicarage.

In 1851 the number of people attending morning service at All Saints' Church was a hundred and ten and in the afternoon a hundred and thirty, with seventy pupils at Sunday school on both occasions. However these were estimated numbers as the vicar objected to making any returns for the ecclesiastical census. It was less likely that he was making a stand against church bureaucracy than that he could not be bothered or that he did not wish to reveal the true figures.

In July 1834, to improve the rear of the Vicarage, (the present-day Glebe House), the Reverend Hood secured a mortgage of £515.8.8d plus interest from the Governors of the Bounty of Queen Anne, which was a fund established in 1704 to supplement the incomes of poor clergy. The loan was conditional on his attending to his duties in the parish, as the Church of England endeavoured to reform itself. The principal and interest were cleared on 15th November 1861.

Education

In 1851 there were 266 children under sixteen, thirty-five per cent of the village population. There were a schoolmaster and three school-mistresses to teach them. Even in 1839 there had been three private schools, with 50-60 pupils, a private evening school and two Sunday schools. For families who could not afford private education a school had been set up inside Nazeing Park, supervised by members of the Palmer family. Eighty places were provided and in 1839 sixty-one children attended.

In 1853 George Palmer died leaving £400 in his will to provide a new school for 'the education of poor persons', so by 1854 the school in Nazeing Park had been replaced. On 7th June that year, at the Court Baron and Customary Court, Sir Charles Wake granted to the Reverend Hood a parcel of waste land, 225ft. by 28ft., at the junction of Hoe Lane and Betts Lane. The school was under the management of the vicar and churchwardens and remained on the site until 1947, when the building passed into private hands. For many years it was known as Dormarlyn Hall and was used for occasional functions. It is now a private residence.

Education was not yet compulsory but almost all children received some schooling. Their attendance depended on whether they were needed to help at home or on the land, so many received only rudimentary teaching. The marriage records for Nazeing between 1847-1851 reveal that a third of the people, ten men and eight women, signed their name with a cross.

Leisure activities

For the majority of Nazeing people work would have taken up most of their waking time. In what leisure time they had, the men at least could resort to the five public houses, neatly positioned round the village, the Crown Hotel at Broxbourne bridge, the King Harold's Head, the Coach and Horses, the Crooked Billet, and the Sun. In addition there were two beersellers, one in Middle Street, the other on Nazeing Common.

Fishermen had access to the River Lea which was noted for its abundance of fish. For subscribers and customers the Crown Hotel had about five miles of river which was stocked annually. The Crown also had "extensive ornamental flower gardens laid out with exquisite taste and effect, and kept up at considerable expense." For those who were

Broxbourne Gardens

A small part of the "extensive ornamental flower gardens" and buildings at the Crown Hotel.

able to afford it, Broxbourne Rowing Club was formed in 1847, with boating in skiffs and punts from the grounds of the Crown Hotel. So, with the arrival of the railway, outsiders were starting to find their way to Nazeing, although very few of the inhabitants would yet have travelled far afield.

The village had been scarcely affected by the industrial and political upheavals of the first half of the nineteenth century; similarly it was not to share fully in the prosperity of the second half. Yet by 1900 there were to be changes afoot which would affect the village in ways which the inhabitants in 1850 could hardly have foreseen.

The Crooked Billet from a photograph taken in the Second World War. It was already a public house by the late 18th century and is now the only one with grazing rights on Nazeingwood Common.

Two postcard views of Nazeingwood Common. Above, in the 1920s, is Abbot's Cottage and the Golf Clubhouse, at the junction of Betts Lane and Common Road. Below are the Cascades which the Palmers had constructed from Nazeing Brook at the boundary of Nazeing Park.

CHAPTER 7

"A PURELY AGRICULTURAL PARISH"

Crisis and recovery, 1851 to 1914

The Great Exhibition of 1851 ushered in a quarter of a century of social and economic prosperity that marked the highpoint of British self-confidence. The worst birth pains of the Industrial Revolution were past and real wages of working people rose substantially. On the land harvests were good and demand from the rapidly growing cities meant that prices were high: people at every level in rural society benefited and the myth of a golden age of stability was created. In the 1870s, however, poor harvests and the rapid development of North American prairie farming combined to throw British agriculture into a deep and prolonged recession, from which it began to emerge only in the years before the First World War.

For Essex the second half of the nineteenth century was disastrous. Initially it did not share fully in the boom because the railways opened up the London market to farmers from further afield and the capital became less reliant on the county for fresh produce. Then it was hit very badly by the slump, particularly in the marginal west Essex wheat growing areas: many farms became derelict and reverted to nature because landlords could not find tenants for them. In 1886 a Parndon tenant farmer told the leading land-agent John Oxley Parker: "The prospects of agriculture grow hopeless day by day, and I can see nothing for it except the poor clay lands be abandoned." This prophecy was soon fulfilled.

Superficially Nazeing altered little in this period. The Palmers and the Burys still owned their big houses and wielded great influence. As late as 1912 the parish council described Nazeing as "a purely agricultural parish". Affected by the depression, its population was almost static. And yet, slowly, change came. Financial problems forced the Palmers to lease out Nazeing Park and the tenant farmers began to play a greater part in village affairs.

George Palmer junior

George Palmer junior (1799-1883) was born in the eighteenth century and lived to see the coming of electric light and the telephone. In 1827 he married Elizabeth Charlotte Surtees, "a handsome, clever and spirited woman ... niece of that Lady Eldon with whom the Chancellor, when a young and poor man, ran away". Their status as gentry did not make them immune to tragedy: their son William died aged only nine months and in 1848 Elizabeth herself died "after giving birth to a daughter who survived her but a short time, leaving three sons and one daughter to mourn their irretrievable loss". The evidence suggests that George too was deeply moved by his bereavement: certainly he never remarried.

When his father died in 1853, George appeared to be inheriting a fine asset. Under the 1861 Nazeing Enclosure Award the family acquired a further 138 acres; by 1872 the Palmer holdings in Nazeing had reached their maximum recorded extent of 801 acres. In the same year, however, financial problems forced George to lease out Nazeing Park so that, with one brief exception, the family never lived there again. In 1858 George himself explained the immediate cause of his difficulties as "the peculiar circumstances under which I have lately been defrauded of a large sum of money." The underlying reasons why he could not simply absorb the blow can be traced back to his father and even his grandfather. His financial difficulties were exacerbated by the level of his own expenditure.

Roundell Palmer, later the 1st Earl of Selborne, as a young MP in 1849. His family papers are an invaluable source of information about the Palmers of Nazeing.

The estate was costly to develop and maintain but it was perhaps above all their sense of public duty, and the accompanying personal expense, that brought the Palmers to crisis point. William and the two Georges were sheriffs of Essex, always an expensive office, and were JPs when that position still carried important administrative as well as judicial functions. George senior fought three expensive parliamentary election campaigns. His brother Jocelyn was glad of his success but "could not rejoice that he was a Member of Parliament" and his nephew Roundell Palmer (Lord Selborne) "doubted whether the honour was worth to him the money it cost".

While seeking to save the estate, George Palmer junior outlined his own record:

> At the time of the great agricultural riots in 1830 ... at the earnest request of the late Lord Melbourne I raised the only corps of yeomanry cavalry in Essex for the especial protection of the Government Gunpowder Manufactury at Waltham Abbey ... I had to maintain it at my own expense for five years but I received no arrears ... I was one of the Commissioners appointed by the House of Commons in 1835 who founded the colony of South Australia without subjecting this nation to one sixpence expense ... I fitted out with others the expedition which made the settlement in New Zealand just 48 hours before the French ...

"A fine old English gentleman" – Lieutenant Colonel George Palmer in the uniform of the West Essex Yeomanry.

The Duke of Wellington twice complimented Palmer as Captain Commandant on the "soldier-like" qualities of the West Essex Yeomanry and in 1847 asked him to mount guards at Tottenham and Bishop's Stortford stations when Queen Victoria and Prince Albert visited Cambridge. This was more than a ceremonial duty, since there had been several attempts on the Queen's life. In 1856, with very little notice, Prince Albert visited the barracks at Colchester and the mayor used the newly invented telegraph to send a message to Nazeing Park. He requested an escort which, led by Sergeant-Major Gray because Palmer was unwell, marched 27 miles cross-country to Chelmsford. They rounded up 21 members of the corps en route, went on the next day to Colchester and back by train, and then marched home, arriving in Waltham Abbey around midnight. In September 1858 the Yeomanry held its annual training manoeuvres on Nazeing Common. Palmer became a Lieutenant-Colonel in 1860 and in 1868 he retired with permission to retain his rank. Army reform and agricultural depression led to a falling off in the number of recruits and on 31st March 1877 the West Essex Yeomanry was disbanded.

The most lasting of George Palmer junior's many achievements was a long and ultimately successful campaign to save Epping Forest from development. In 1842 he was elected as a Verderer of the Forest, which in itself probably cost hundreds of pounds. Soon afterwards, with the coming of the railways, attempts were made to sell off large parts of the forest for housing development, so, in 1863, the House of Commons established a Select Committee on Royal Forests to investigate the issue. From the outset Palmer had strenuously opposed these sales; he asserted in his evidence to the Committee that Londoners' recreational use of the forest was "a prescriptive right, a right which they have exercised for eight hundred years past - from time immemorial ... provided they behaved themselves". He claimed that he was "protecting the rights of the Poorer Foresters who are unable to protect themselves", and risked ostracism by Sir Charles Wake and others of his own class when he attacked "encroachments wilfully made by the lords of the manor". His priorities were to "secure the rights of the Sovereign, an open space for exercising troops and the recreation of the humbler classes", and he lived to see Queen Victoria dedicate Epping Forest to the public in 1882. Later the cause was taken up by others who are now better remembered but, writing within living memory of these events, Edward Hardingham commented that "Lieut.-Colonel George was ... a fine old English gentleman who did his best to preserve the forest ... single-handed at the last".

For reasons that are unclear, George Palmer believed that he was entitled to personal recompense for the enclosures that did take place but his plea, in 1858, that compensation "would be most acceptable to me at the present time" was ignored and he was forced into drastic action. First he borrowed £45,000 on the security of the estate; then he put it up for auction but found no buyer. In 1866 he sold a property at Much Hadham which had been in the family for at least sixty years and, soon afterwards, he moved to Hubbards, where he was rather sadly described as a "boarder". This was still not enough. In 1871 Nazeing Park was occupied by Mrs Sarah Cook, who described her occupation as "In charge of Nazeing Park Mansion". The following year it was let to Robert Henty Esq. on a fourteen year lease, a type of arrangement which was already becoming commonplace because it enabled poor gentry to obtain an income from their property without giving it up entirely.

In 1873 the whole estate was put up for auction by Edward Duckett, who now held the mortgage. The highest bidder was George's youngest son, Ralph Charlton Palmer, who paid £47,000. There was something slightly curious about this transaction, which is indicated by a tantalising

A hunt meeting at the King Harold's Head in about 1910.

but uncorroborated note in the Mercers' Company archive which states that George was "turned out of his house by a conspiracy of his children, a [illegible] and a lawyer". In 1877 George, "upwards of 77 years of age and too infirm to manage my own affairs", gave his eldest son a power of attorney to manage them for him.

In 1849 George had been the central character in another conflict with the Wakes. He arranged a meeting of stag hounds over Nazeing Common which was attended by about a hundred spectators. Just as the riders were about to set out from the King Harold's Head, Phillipson, bailiff to Sir Charles Wake, tried to prevent them because they would be trespassing on Wake's property. George told Phillipson that as "a Verderer of Epping Forest and the Holder of a Forest Deputation" he would "authorise the hunt under the Crown". He carried on with the meet, so Phillipson acknowledged defeat and joined in. Sir Charles, acting through his solicitor, took Palmer to court for trespassing on the Common and shooting game there, so George's conveyancer brother William carried out painstaking archival research into the history of the Common. He established conclusively that "the Common was a very peculiar common" which the Earl of Carlisle had granted to the villagers in 1651, and the case against George was thrown out. William rediscovered also the obligation of the lords of the manor to provide at Nazeing Bury "a Bull, a Boar and a Stallion for the use of the villagers", and noted that they had for many years neglected this duty.

This is the first recorded episode in which the resident Palmers openly championed the villagers against the absentee Wakes and it may mark a significant change in village attitudes toward the Palmers, from respect to affection. It was not uncommon for paternalist Tory gentry to soften the effects of the new Poor Law or even to refuse to implement it. The fact that the 1851 census shows 21 people drawing parish relief in Nazeing, rather than being banished to the Epping workhouse, may suggest that George and his father took this line, at least with those who were suitably deferential. Perhaps sympathy for his personal losses, first of his wife and two youngest children, then of his house, together with support for his stand over Epping Forest, produced within Nazeing an affection for George Palmer which in his pomp he could never have achieved.

Ralph Charlton Palmer

Ralph (1839-1923) was George junior's youngest son and followed in the footsteps of his cousin Roundell Palmer, to Winchester, Oxford,

Lincoln's Inn, and the Bar. In 1872 Roundell was created Earl of Selborne and appointed Lord Chancellor, in which office he was responsible for the building of the Royal Courts of Justice in the Strand. Selborne continued to keep a benevolent eye on Ralph's progress and between 1880 and 1885 appointed him to three different posts. This was mild nepotism, undoubtedly, but it was after the opening up of the Civil Service to competitive examination and Ralph would have used his legal training, so he probably obtained his posts on merit as well. As the youngest son of one of the minor gentry, recently impoverished, he certainly

Roundell Palmer, 1st Earl of Selborne, in his robes as the Lord Chancellor.

needed the money. Selborne had many fine qualities but a sense of humour was not the most conspicuous of them, so his comment that Ralph was "well qualified" for his post in the Lunacy Office is unlikely to have been a cousinly tease. Ralph was at various times Secretary to the Public Schools Commission, Deputy Chairman of the City and Guilds Institute, and a member of the Senate of London University.

Although in 1873 Ralph and his older brother Archdale Villiers Palmer bought back the estate, the family never again enjoyed full possession of it. To pay for it they had to raise a mortgage for £35,000, which was not cleared until 1924. They returned to Nazeing Park for a few years in the 1890s but then moved out again. By 1908 the tenant was Walter Hargreaves, a wealthy Lloyds underwriter who soon became a leading figure in Nazeing.

Ralph Palmer, who for half a century played a major part in village affairs, including the building of the new road which was "first and foremost an improvement for the solitary parish of Nazeing".

Oscar Wilde's Lady Bracknell complained that "land gives one position and prevents one from keeping it up", a comment which describes how the slump ruined many minor gentry. Ralph Palmer avoided this fate, supplementing his income as a senior civil servant by running the estate with knowledge and enthusiasm for fifty years. Soon after taking over from his father as Treasurer of Nazeing Wood or Park in

1877, his enthusiasm ran away with him and he was "fined a sum to be assessed by the Trustees other than himself for having encroached on the Common by depositing timber thereon". Although he employed a bailiff, he was described as a farmer in the trades section of some issues of Kelly's directory. For a few years he lived at Lodge Farm. While there he built a new track to Common Road which cost probably around £250, so evidently he had weathered the worst of the financial storm.

The case of Brewitts Farm shows that Palmer took drastic action towards making the estate pay. He turned the neighbouring Shepherds Farm into two cottages (now Northside and The Cottage) and added the land from Shepherds and four other fields to Brewitts, increasing its acreage from 65 to 117. He converted twenty acres of the enlarged Brewitts from arable to pasture, which was less labour-intensive. To make the farm a more attractive proposition, Palmer included the common rights, each worth an estimated £3 10s per annum, from three nearby cottages. It was predominantly laid to grass and the tenancy agreement went into great detail, including a requirement to "manure annually one fourth of the pasture land at least with eight good cart-loads of well-made farm manure per acre".

Often such provisions were added by a bailiff or an attorney but Palmer probably insisted on this one himself. An impoverished squire forced to earn a living through a profession, he was visited around 1900 by another of the same ilk whose chosen trade was writing. Rider Haggard was an enthusiastic and conscientious gentleman-farmer, best known for the rather lurid African romances such as *King Solomon's Mines* which subsidised his Norfolk estate, but who also wrote a book called *Rural England* in which he reported that

> Mr Palmer, a gentleman noted for his great skill as a judge of Hereford and other cattle at the larger agricultural shows ... had some beautiful Herefords ... and a bullock of two and a half years which was a positive monster ... [His] farming was excellent, and of barley especially he grew very heavy crops per acre. It was not his custom to use artificial manure, as he preferred to rely upon large dressings of farmyard muck.

The land policies of the 1906 Liberal government brought many properties onto the market but Lloyd George, the Chancellor of the Exchequer, was often the excuse owners had been looking for rather than the real reason. Apparently Ralph Palmer had no difficulty in keeping his estate intact. As the worst of the depression passed, his fortunes probably improved and between 1913 and 1920, assisted by his nephew Archdale, he paid off £20,000 of his mortgage.

The Burys

The Burys experienced no financial problems comparable to those of the Palmers; indeed, they remained in possession of St. Leonards until the 1960s. It is perhaps for this reason that less is recorded about them, although we do know that they too suffered a succession of personal tragedies. James Frederick Bury (1798-1860), who inherited the estate in 1825, lost his nineteen year old daughter Augusta in February 1854 and her fourteen year old sister Selina six months later. The eldest son of Charles James (1831-1897) died aged eight days and his second son at the age of thirteen.

James Frederick Bury. He inherited the family's estate in 1825.

Charles James Bury,

and his wife Anne.

Charles James Bury was for many years on the Board of Guardians of the Poor and in 1894 was elected unopposed as Nazeing's first Epping Rural District councillor. When, in 1897, he died suddenly the chairman of the Board commented: "He was a man who never spared himself and I cannot help feeling he has shortened his life by his devotion to his work". The parish council paid tribute to "the energy and ability displayed by the late Mr. Bury in the discharge of his parochial duties".

Ralph Frederic Bury inherited the St. Leonards estate on 13th December 1897, nine days before his 21st birthday. He was a young man of great energy and by the age of 25 was a barrister at Lincoln's Inn, a J.P. and a district councillor. He and Archdale Palmer are remembered by many older Nazeing residents; whereas Palmer began to play a major part in village affairs only in the 1920s, Bury was already involved in the 1890s. Like Ralph Palmer, he managed his estate actively. At least four buildings bear his initials and the date of their construction, Salem/Riddens View (1900), a stable at Nether Kidders (1904), and two houses near the junction of St. Leonards Road and Laundry Lane (1909 and 1936). Bury listed farming as one of his recreations and, unlike Ralph Palmer, was willing to try out artificial fertilisers. Working with the county council, he carried out a series of experiments which were described in some detail by Rider Haggard, who concluded that, in this case at least, the artificial manure produced better results. In 1910, at the

St Leonards, the home of the Bury family until the 1960s. From a photograph of around 1900.

exceptionally young age of 34, Bury became High Sheriff of Essex, a ceremonial but still important office that was of more than normal significance in the year of a coronation, at which he participated as Gold Rod Officer.

The Chapel

In 1887 Augustus Jessopp, the rector of Scarning in Norfolk, wrote:

> the stuffy little chapel by the wayside ... has been the only place where the peasantry have enjoyed the free expression of their opinions and where, under an organisation elaborated with extraordinary sagacity, they have kept up a school of music, literature, politics and eloquence, self-supporting and unaided by dole or subsidy ...

Augustus was the youngest son of John Sympson Jessopp, who eighty years earlier had denounced the "pretensions" of William Palmer over the disputed common rights. He may even have known Nazeing Chapel, which was in many respects a typical example of his descriptions. Its leaders were mostly comfortably off farmers who themselves employed several men: the most prominent of them were the Pegrums.

For at least four centuries there had been Pegrums in Nazeing, most of them respectable but unobtrusive tenant farmers and religious nonconformists. During the 1850s four of the family became eligible for the then very limited electoral franchise, James Pegrum who farmed 54 acres at Perry Hill, Samuel (74 at Ninnings), Joseph senior (190 at Greenleaves), and Abraham (36 at Darmers). All qualified as "occupiers of land" rather than as landowners but since their landlord was the absentee Edward Williams, their influence was considerable. James, who was known as "Peg-leg" because he had only one leg, led the chapel singing, often using an accordion. At Ninnings Samuel hosted "booth meetings", a festive outdoor summer celebration of the church's anniversary.

The slow rise of the chapel accelerated in 1860 with the arrival at Cheshunt College of a new President, Henry Reynolds. He encouraged the chapels in the college's care towards greater self-sufficiency and instituted a scheme whereby a senior student, known as a dean, took

**About 1880. On the right is Hannah, wife of James "Pegleg"
Pegrum, who occupied Perry Hill Farm for more than 40 years.**

responsibility for each one. In 1861 a special meeting at Nazeing Chapel adopted new rules and for the first time three deacons were elected to manage its affairs: they were Joseph Pegrum senior (who was also the treasurer), farmer Thomas Nicholls of Parvills in Epping Upland, and William Welch, a farmer and shoemaker who lived at Curtis Farm.

With congregations increasing, the first chapel was clearly too small so, in 1876, it was taken down and replaced by the present building, which cost about £900. Most prominent in the subscription list are the Pegrum and Nicholls families, with other notable village names such as Argent, Dean, Standingford, Welch, Judd, and Coleman also represented. The Burys of St. Leonards made a modest contribution but the name of Palmer was conspicuous by its absence. It was by no means a purely local effort and the three largest contributions came from outside, £100 from the Countess of Huntingdon's Connexion, £50 from the Liberal M.P. and leading nonconformist Samuel Morley, and £50 from the philanthropist Sir Titus Salt.

The brothers Joseph and James Pegrum died within a week of each other in 1888. Joseph was the first person to be buried at All Saints'

Sixty-two members of the Pegrum family at Nazeing Bury on the occasion of Susannah Pegrum's 50th birthday in 1897. She and her husband Joseph are in the centre of the group.

without a service's being held there and the chapel members, numbed by their loss, erected a plaque in his memory. In the same year the chapel was authorised for the registration of marriages. The first wedding was between Elizabeth Head and George Lipson, who was for many years the secretary to the chapel and clerk to the parish council.

Joseph was succeeded as deacon and treasurer by his son Joseph, who was clearly a man of considerable drive and ability. At the age of only 25 he was the tenant of Sir Herewald Wake at Nazeing Bury, the largest farm in the village; by 1900 he was farming a total of 600 acres. When Rider Haggard was researching *Rural England*, his plan was to visit the leading landholders in each place, so naturally he visited Palmer and Bury; it is an indication of Joseph Pegrum's influence that Haggard visited him also. Pegrum was at various times an Overseer of the Poor, a district and parish councillor, and a trustee of the Nazeing Wood or Park.

The chapel undertook a series of evangelistic missions to bring the Gospel to the village, and within twenty years almost a hundred people had become church members. In 1903 the Welsh Revival broke out and the dean at the time, Harland Brine, asked: "If in Wales, why not in Nazeing?" Such was the effect of the mission that year that the Crooked Billet was closed on a Saturday night and a good number of people were converted. Among them was George Hutchings, who had been dismissed as pindar of the Common for embezzlement and developed a reputation as one of the most irreligious men in the village before turning to God at the age of 63. The episode is described vividly by Harland Brine in a little pamphlet entitled *The Old Shepherd*.

Perhaps the most endearing of the deans was the whole-hearted Welshman, Robert Davies. At a time when "muscular Christianity" was more associated with Anglicanism than nonconformity, he founded the chapel football team and played for it with enthusiastic abandon at centre half. Notoriously absent-minded, he turned up at one match to find that he had brought one football boot and one carpet-slipper. Robert was even late for his own wedding. Immaculately dressed in black morning coat and striped trousers, he was collected from Broxbourne station by Joseph Pegrum who took him along to the chapel in his tub-cart. As the horse pulled up the hill near Mansion House Farm, the shafts slipped out of the saddle and the chapel's two leading figures were deposited unceremoniously on the dusty gravel road.

Not all at the chapel was sweetness and light. Having developed its independence, it had a long struggle with Cheshunt College to get control

The Coleman family at Darmers in the 1880s. Although they were sub-tenants of the Pegrums for nearly 50 years, there was some tension between the families.

of its own trust deeds; this was not achieved until 1932. In 1905 Harland Brine reported that, despite taking the pledge, Thomas Pegrum was repeatedly drunk. It was agreed therefore to suspend him from church membership for six months, a sanction which was sadly ineffective because Thomas later drowned in the water on the Common. At times there were other conflicts such as the tensions between the Pegrums and the Colemans, who came later on the chapel scene and as sub-tenants of the Pegrums were rather lower down the subtly graded class structure of the village.

In the early 1900s the very success of the chapel was itself a cause of some contention. Greatly increased numbers of children at the Sunday School meant that larger premises were needed. George Lipson, who was Sunday School superintendent as well as secretary, complained that "nobody outside those interested in the Sunday School care whether we have a better building or not". His threat in February 1908 to "retire from the whole thing" if something were not started soon may have had the desired effect, since a new hall was started later in 1908 and opened in May 1909. A few years later, however, Lipson resigned over some issue tantalisingly referred to but not specifically mentioned in the chapel minutes.

The successes nevertheless outweighed the failures and the opening of the Sunday School hall demonstrated that the chapel had become a force to be reckoned with. As was the custom among the free churches at the time, leading contributors were invited to lay donor stones. They included not only prominent chapel names such as Pegrum, Lipson, Welch, and Banks but also two rather more unexpected ones - Walter Hargreaves, who had leased Nazeing Park recently and was perhaps seeking to make an impact in the village, and Ralph Palmer who, 30 years earlier, had failed to contribute to the building of the main chapel.

The participation of Palmer and Hargreaves indicates one important respect in which Nazeing Chapel did not entirely conform to the portrait painted by Augustus Jessopp. The leaders of many country chapels used the skills he described as a springboard for positions of responsibility in agricultural trade unions or radical politics but in west Essex these movements had little influence. Nazeing Chapel was an essentially conservative organisation and its leaders seem to have won the respect of the gentry and became a part of the establishment without compromising their religious principles too much. Even William Welch, who as a shoemaker belonged to a trade which often produced political radicals, was married to a Pegrum and displayed no subversive tendencies. Members of the chapel congregation were influential in the village. At least seven were elected as parish councillors and five were Trustees of the Common.

The Church

Although the Church of England made vigorous attempts to reform itself during the nineteenth century, in Nazeing it did not grow as rapidly as the Chapel. The vicars were usually resident and apparently conscientious enough but most of them were in their fifties when appointed and were perhaps given a quiet rural parish for the autumn of their careers. In 1865 Elisha Hood was succeeded by Rowland Smith, who was for five years a Trustee of the Common, the only vicar to have undertaken this office. He wrote extensively on church law but neither he nor Hood did much to improve the fabric of All Saints', so that when Henry M. Tyrwhitt arrived in 1872 he was appalled by its damp and neglected condition. He initiated a major restoration of the building and in 1878 the organ was installed at a cost of £170. Robert P. Waller (1879-90) was recorded in 1884 as holding morning and afternoon services every Sunday, with additional evening services in summer and Communion twice a month and on feast-days.

In 1890 Waller exchanged livings with Thomas Ward Goddard of Bitteswell near Rugby. Goddard was an active, if sometimes

The Reverend Thomas Goddard going to church on his 82nd birthday, Sunday, 9th September, 1917.

controversial, vicar who retired in 1923, shortly before his death at the age of 88. Goddard continued with the restoration, building the vestry, installing the chancel arch, repairing the roof, and improving the Vicarage. In 1899 his daughter Alice Mary Fane died, aged only 32, and the present pulpit was given in her memory. In the same year the church spire was removed, presumably because it was unsafe.

The creation in 1894 of elected parish councils throughout the country meant that it was necessary to separate the civil and ecclesiastical functions of the parish. At first this was very amicable in Nazeing: the church offered the use of the vestry for parish council meetings, although the offer was declined in favour of the Board School. Thomas Goddard was elected to the first parish council and made some useful contributions. Then, in the 1896 election, he tied with chapel deacon John Davies Welch for the last place on the council and seems to have withdrawn in something of a huff. He stood again in 1901 but was not elected, perhaps because the nonconformists used their influence to keep him out or because he was a rather prickly character.

In 1902 there arose a far from amicable dispute, which may have been aggravated by the vicar's unfortunate experiences with the parish council. He had received from the Board of Agriculture a Certificate of Redemption of Tithe of Non-Ecclesiastical Property in Nazeing, which the parish council claimed that he should have handed to them; he refused on the grounds that he did not have the Board's permission. The parish council then requested that the vicar should give them also the original 1847 Tithe Award documents, a motion proposed by John Banks and Joseph Pegrum, which may indicate that there was no love lost between Church and Chapel. The Essex Local Government Committee suggested that the Tithe Award should be kept in the vestry. The parish council replied in a long and closely-argued letter that the vestry was no more than a robing-room and not a suitable place to keep the Award, particularly as the vicar regarded the church as his freehold and had refused access contrary to the Parish Councils Act. Goddard replied that the letter was "terribly inaccurate" and "hazarded the conjecture" that it had been drafted by Ralph Palmer, who was also a churchwarden. The vicar added that access to the church was never denied and that the map had been used only three times in his thirteen years as incumbent. The committee confirmed its previous decision that the award and map should be kept in the vestry. Perhaps the First World War put these petty disputes into their true perspective, for in 1919 there was close co-operation between Goddard and the chapel leaders over the provision of a war memorial.

Agriculture, employment, and housing

Nazeing broadly followed the national pattern of boom, depression and recovery. Between 1851 and 1871 there was a small increase in population, from 757 to 786. Many English tenant farmers enjoyed a comfortable life, often aping the manners of the gentry and separating themselves from their men. Whether this happened in Nazeing is unknown; certainly few farms changed hands, an indicator that they were doing fairly well, so probably the village enjoyed a modest share of the national prosperity.

Nazeing was undoubtedly affected by the slump. Between 1871 and 1881 the population dropped by over six per cent, to 738, its lowest level since 1820. In the 1880s Ralph Palmer and Charles Bury avoided the fate of many gentry by hard work and effective consolidation of their estates but there was a greater turnover of tenant farmers than before, perhaps because they could not adapt to the harsher economic climate. Ralph Bury, writing to the *Nazeing Parish Magazine* in 1932, described the fate of the "Old Mill", which he remembered:

> It was never of great fame and was allowed to fall into disrepair, because as land was laid to grass it gradually ceased to be remunerative. The same applies ... to others in this neighbourhood as they were common to every village 100 years ago. I don't suppose it ever occurred to anyone to have a picture made of it ...

Many Essex landowners responded by switching to livestock farming, which was less labour-intensive, and recruited experienced dairy farmers from Scotland and the west country, who noticed the difference in attitude and referred to themselves as "working farmers" but the natives as "collar and tie farmers". At least three farmers moved to Nazeing from the west country and Will Graham came from Ayrshire to Harolds Park Farm, where he rapidly established an extensive milk-round. There is no record of their thoughts about what they found. Families such as the Pegrums, brought up in the nonconformist tradition of hard work, did make the required adjustment, although they were not necessarily happy about it. Joseph told Haggard that "to earn a living a farmer had to work like a labourer". Despite the difficulties, the picture in Nazeing was less gloomy than in the nation at large, probably because it had always been an area of mixed farming and was therefore able to switch the emphasis from arable to dairy more easily. In the 1880s the number of agricultural labourers dropped by only ten per cent and there was actually one more farmer, whereas in the country as a whole numbers fell by a third and a quarter respectively.

Throughout England it had long been the right of cottagers to graze stock on riverside meadows and roadside verges, an untidy custom which was seen by the early Victorian official mind as waste in every sense of the word. Enclosure awards enabled landowners to gobble up small parcels of land next to their existing property, while the poorer commoners received no compensation for losses which could be of vital importance in their subsistence economy. Middle Street, for example, was formerly up to 100 yards wide in parts; the former edge of the road can be seen at older houses such as Goodalls and Ninnings. The enclosed waste area was so great that new houses such as Rose Cottage and Little Dormers could be built on it. Most significant, however, was the enclosure of the marsh and the mead, almost 400 acres of rich grazing land where commoners had valuable rights called cowleazes. The Palmers acquired 138 acres, the Wakes 84, and the Burys 47. Altogether around 450 acres were enclosed, over one tenth of the village.

In 1885 William Westall reported in *The Spectator* the assertion of an old resident that, "before the poor were despoiled by the lords of the manor", the cottagers had pastured their geese on the greens and "they were so well-off that in order to levy a rate the rate-payers had to 'make a pauper'". "Now," he added bitterly, "there are paupers in plenty". Even allowing for the human propensity to locate a lost golden age some twenty years in the past, there would seem to be some truth in this statement. It would indicate another factor contributing to the local hardship of the period, and may suggest that George Palmer junior was less enthusiastic about the rights of commoners when his own interests were affected. Further investigation of this apparently minor topic could well shed new light on the most obscure period of nineteenth-century Nazeing history.

Westall goes on to paint a vivid portrait of Nazeing agriculture. One large farm, (unnamed, but possibly Harolds Park before the coming of Will Graham), was untenanted because it had been "brought into such a condition by neglect and bad management that nobody would buy the hay, which is the only thing it produces". Hay was the main crop in Nazeing and, since demand was fairly constant, the better the harvest the greater the profit. One farmer, who had made only £117 the previous year, expected to make nearly £500 in the best year since 1875. Rents were high and, with rates and tithes anything up to 10s per acre, a poor harvest could be disastrous. Carting hay to London was an important local business but not very profitable. The carter would set off at 3pm and arrive at Whitechapel Market at seven the next morning. Later on he had to deliver the hay to the buyer, so often he did not get back to Nazeing till the following day. He received only 12s per journey and seldom had the opportunity to make extra money by bringing a load back so, with three journeys a week, he had only 36s to provide for himself, his family, his horse, and his expenses.

An agricultural labourer's wages were only about 12s per week and farm work was in decline as an occupation. During the boom some landlords and farmers sought to increase productivity and counter high wage demands by investing in machinery; in 1871 a steam cultivator was taken to and from Harold's Park Farm over the Common. This, however, was such a major event that it was remembered 35 years later, so it seems unlikely that there was much mechanisation, except perhaps when the slump began to ease after 1900.

When Rider Haggard visited Nazeing, he asked his three interviewees whether they could find labourers. Ralph Palmer and Ralph Bury both had enough, although Palmer added that "the men must be handled carefully". Joseph Pegrum complained that "it was difficult to find skilled labour, or to find a lad who would learn ploughing." Pegrum told Haggard that he had no cottages for his labourers and showed him where they lived:

> ... a brick shed, measuring twelve or fourteen feet square, which might have served as a wagon house and was, I think I am right in saying, windowless. In this place, upon sacks that lay around the wall, slept the twenty men upon the floor. No washing apparatus was visible and no fireplace.

Haggard described the problem of labour shortages as "universal", but if these conditions were typical it was scarcely surprising.

Pegrum and other village leaders did little to remedy the deficiency. In 1897 the parish council asked a Mr. Lawrence to "desist taking water from Clappers Weir [by the bottom of Perry Hill] for his building operations in Middle Street". Perhaps as a result of relief measures which would have made the area less vulnerable to flooding, building began by the Lea, at Riverside. In 1910 Ralph Bury complained to the district council about a

Alfred Coleman, an agricultural labourer. He was the tenant at Darmers from the 1870s until his death in 1922. From a photograph of about 1900.

"bungalow craze" which "tended to depreciate values and would soon need special sewage". The sanitary inspector visited the site where he found seven bungalows and five houses which were "well-built and artistic and could have costs hundreds of pounds". They "definitely were not shanties" and there was good local sanitation so the matter was dropped.

In 1908 Dr John Wells, who ran a well-known medical practice in Hoddesdon and Nazeing, bought Tylers Cross Farm, 250 acres of mixed farmland at Broadley Common. A few years later he offered to provide land for cottages there but the parish council declined the offer. They declared that Nazeing was "a purely agricultural parish" and added that there were "upwards of 40 cottages in Upper Nazeing", available for agricultural labourers", so that there was no demand "in excess of the supply or beyond what may be obtained by agreement".

Although families were large and most children survived to adulthood, the net population between 1851 and 1914 remained almost static. The census of 1891 shows noticeably greater mobility of employment, probably a direct result of the slump. Many younger people moved to London, which doubled in population in the second half of the nineteenth century; others may have got casual work there while continuing to live in Nazeing. A substantial minority of those who remained in the village were employed outside, including workers who walked to the Waltham Abbey Gunpowder Factory and clerks who commuted by railway via Broxbourne to the City. Some of the 22 professional people may have been refugees from London, moving in the opposite direction to seek a more rural environment. As twentieth century censuses are published it will be possible to trace how the trickle of 1891 became a flood which made natives of Nazeing a minority in their own village.

Nazeingwood Common

After the teething troubles of the forty years following the 1778 Act, Nazeing Wood or Park settled down to a century of comparative calm, although it was not without its problems.

In 1847 the pindar, John Harknett, failed by his own admission to account for £2 7s 6d in fees. George Palmer senior, as treasurer, and the other trustees deducted the money from his wages, deciding that he must "be dismissed pindar" and quit his tied cottage within three months. Harknett stayed but in January 1848 was thrown out, not the ideal time of year for his wife and four children, whatever his misdemeanours. He moved to Roydon but later slipped back across the parish boundary to rustle Palmer's sheep, before fleeing to his brother in Surrey. Palmer, acting as a Justice of the Peace, instructed the Nazeing constable to pursue and arrest him. Harknett was sentenced to transportation but, perhaps because he was already 55 years old, the punishment was commuted to a short spell of imprisonment in England.

Thirty years later there was a very similar episode. Perhaps because the trustees were suspicious that something was amiss, they gave the pindar, George Hutchings, a cheque book [receipt book], which he was to produce at the Annual General Meeting, showing the number of sheep and cattle turned on to the Common and the name of the person paying for them. They discovered several discrepancies in accounts, with a total deficit of £11 18s, and resolved that "The shepherd leave the service of the trust and quit the Pindar's cottage on 1 January unless he explained the foregoing circumstances to the satisfaction of the Trustees." No reply was forthcoming, so that the obvious explanation is that he had embezzled the money. Shortly afterwards George Palmer junior and Abraham Bull resigned as trustees, both indicating that infirmity precluded their carrying out their duties. This was not unreasonable, given that both were nearly eighty, but it was unusual for trustees to resign halfway through the year. Maybe they felt some degree of responsibility, perhaps by neglect.

Taking over as treasurer, Ralph Palmer found the trustees' finances at a low ebb. The starting of a new minute book specifically for the trustees' business and the immediate abolition of their traditional annual dinner (which had cost £2) suggest that Ralph had a more business-like approach. Soon Nazeing Wood or Park came into profit. With his encouragement, a cricket club and golf links were established on the Common, although in 1891 John Banks won a vote that "there should be no games on the common without the consent of the majority of Common Right owners". In 1893, however, permission for golf was granted, "Mr Banks alone dissenting". The rent of £37 (10s per member) more than offset what would otherwise have been a loss on the year for the trust and probably explains why the right-holders changed their minds. The club was soon firmly established, so that only ten years after its foundation the course was noted by Rider Haggard as "well-known".

Haggard was less impressed by the Common itself. It was "covered with tens of thousands of ant-heaps that greatly damage, if they do not ruin, the pasture, while the surrounding land is practically free of these

Nazeing Common Golf Club. "Approach to the 14th Green."

"Probably one of the best of links within 20 miles of London", where golf was played first in 1890. The course survived until Nazeing Common was ploughed up in 1941. From a postcard dated 1913.

pests". He attributed the problem to the multiple ownership, which meant that "What is everybody's business is nobody's business, therefore the emmet-heaps remain unlevelled". The suggestion may not be entirely fair because the whole area around the Common was infested by moles and one field at Lodge Farm has long been called Molehilly Field. Several generations of the Harknett family, who lived next to the gate at the top of the Common and gave it their name, were molecatchers, and Ralph Bury often went out mole catching with the last of them.

Haggard did not perhaps discuss the Common with his host because in 1907 it was stated that "The management of the Common has to a great extent been left in the hands of Ralph Charlton Palmer ... the Chairman of the Management Trustees". This comment was made in the course of the Palmer v Guadagni court case, one which had remarkable parallels with that of Standingford v. Palmer 70 years earlier. In 1894 Ralph Palmer wrote to William Graham, tenant of Harold's Park Farm, warning him that his "action in crossing the Common with carts was a trespass which the Trustees would not further permit". The matter rumbled on for another ten years until finally, in April 1904, the trustees had had enough and Palmer warned Graham: "If you break down the fence we will commence proceedings ..." The owner of Harold's Park Farm, an Italian nobleman named Guitto Guadagni, asserted through his agent that "there was no other way of getting timber from The Copse [Copy Wood] and the owner had always had a right to cart it through one of the Common Gates". The Trustees offered arbitration, which was refused, so they determined to take the matter further.

Whereas Standingford v Palmer had for convenience been heard at the King Harold's Head, the railway now made it easy for witnesses to get to the High Court. The case came before Mr Justice Swinfen Eady on 17th to 20th July 1907. The two sides sought to demonstrate whether or not there was a custom of carting on the Common and, as in 1838, called witnesses whose evidence gives us a valuable picture of daily life in Nazeing. One of them was George Hutchings, who stated that he "gave up the pindar's post 30 years ago", a slightly different interpretation of events from that of the trustees. The judge found that the defendants had a good case over Copy Wood but rejected their claims to the right of carting from three other fields. The trustees won £3 13s 8d in damages but it was a pyrrhic victory because each side had to bear its own costs. Theirs totalled £439 16s, creating a debt which took twenty years to clear.

The Pindar's House was rebuilt in 1901 as the Trustees had been paying big repair bills. This photograph from the 1930s shows the pindar, William Hampton and his son John.

It is ironical that Ralph Palmer, who had done so much to put Nazeing Wood or Park on a sound financial footing, left it with such a burden.

In 1898 Joseph Pegrum had been elected as a Trustee of Nazeing Wood or Park, defeating Ralph Palmer's nephew Archdale in the one of the few contested elections. Archdale was elected in 1903 but, when in the same year Ralph Palmer stood down temporarily, it was Pegrum who acted as chairman to the trust. Shortly afterwards Joseph's fellow Congregationalist John Banks was elected as a trustee. There was a curious little episode when the trustees turned down a request for the Essex Imperial Yeomanry to cross the Common on its way to its camp at North Weald. The newspaper report of the decision added cryptically that "The Trustees ... Ralph Palmer J.P., presiding, were not unanimous in refusing permission" and it would be interesting to know how the vote divided. Banks had already opposed the golf course and many nonconformists were against the Boer War, in which Archdale Palmer had served with distinction as a captain: it seems likely, therefore, that either Ralph Palmer or the other trustee, Ralph Bury, voted with Pegrum and Banks against his fellow-gentry. When Joseph retired through ill health after 33 years as a trustee, a special vote of thanks for his work was passed.

Crime and punishment

The rise of the Chapel and the continuing presence of the Palmers and Burys as resident JPs ensured that Nazeing people were mostly law-abiding and that their misdemeanours were comparatively minor. Farmer Thomas Webb, for example, was fined 5s for "riding asleep and without a light". In some cases they were convicted for offences related to trade with London, as when haycarter Albert Sampson was fined 2s 6d for leaving the employ of farmer Isaac Hale without notice, so that Hale lost the sale of a load of hay that Sampson was to have taken to Spitalfields. More seriously, John Osler, a farmer and butcher of Denver Lodge, was found guilty of selling diseased meat to the Central Meat Market at Smithfield and fined the substantial sum of £50 plus costs.

Improved communications, however, gave greater opportunities for outsiders to come into the village and cause trouble. In 1895, for example, a group of youths from Hoddesdon were fined for using abusive language in Nazeing. One of them, William Littlechild, was given 21 days' hard labour for assaulting Silas Challis and the presiding JP,

Charles Bury, declared that "the Bench were determined to make an example of the defendant after the disgraceful scenes which took place in Nazing last week". Curiously, another of the youths, Robert Clark, assaulted George Standingford by punching his head but escaped much more lightly, paying a 5s fine with 10s 6d costs. In 1898 Alfred Curtis of Dalston was fined £2 with 10s 6d costs for trespassing in search of conies on land occupied by William Graham and on Easter Monday 1901, at the Crooked Billet, "a gang of youths from Bethnal Green interfered with passers-by".

The Common was a favourite target, perhaps because the culprits thought the chances of being caught were as remote as the Common itself. John Banks, for example, "warned off would-be poachers & London Bird Catchers". The landlords of the Sun and the Lion and Lamb (a small beerhouse in the row of cottages between the Sun and Harknetts Gate) informed the trustees that they had "requested the police to assist in preventing the incursion of beanfeasters". On the morning of Sunday 1st December 1912 there was a typical episode. The pindar, Henry Gentry, found a hare in a snare and took it to the clerk to the trustees, Walter Brown, who watched through his field-glasses and saw four men with four dogs come onto the Common and spread out with the evident intention of beating up game. Having arranged for P.C. Wedlock to go towards Epping Green, Brown rode across the Common on his horse and rounded two of the men up himself, while the other two "ran into the arms of the constable". Afterwards Brown found snares and freshly killed rabbits near where he had seen the men, who were tried at Epping Petty Sessions. Herbert Smith of Thornwood "had a bad record" and was fined 20s, while Leonard Smith of Thornwood and Alfred Nash of Harlow Common were fined 10s. Daniel Brown junior of Epping Upland also committed a similar offence on the land of Charles Pegrum at Nazeing but was a young man of previous good character and so he was bound over and "put under the Probation Officer".

Leisure and recreation

The second half of the nineteenth century saw an increase in the amount of leisure time and greater formalisation in the way it was used. For working people the most popular sports were cricket in the summer and football in the winter. Nazeing Cricket Club was formed in 1883 and in the early 1900s Robert Davies started the Congregational Chapel's football and cricket teams, which played on Joseph Pegrum's land at

Langfield. There must have been other teams with differing degrees of formal organisation for which no records have survived.

Broxbourne Rowing Club had been formed in 1847. Around 1860 the first boathouse was built near to the Crown. In 1897 the club affiliated to the Amateur Rowing Association and built a second clubhouse at a cost of £450, funded by the issue of debentures. When it burnt down in 1905 it was rebuilt on the same site in six weeks, at a cost of £600. Access was only with the permission of the landlord of the Crown, at a cost of one guinea per annum, and rowing in outrigged boats was not allowed on Sundays.

Golf was growing rapidly in popularity throughout the country. In 1890 the newly arrived vicar, Thomas Goddard, with the support of Ralph Palmer, founded the Golf Club on Nazeing Common. He showed the choir boys, some of whom acted as caddies on the course, how to handle golf clubs and for many years acted as the honorary secretary. In 1902 Kelly's Directory stated:

> There are good golf-links of 18 holes, extending over nearly 3 miles of ground on Nazeing Common, and probably one of the best of the links within 20 miles of London. The club is limited to 200 members and has its own clubhouse and dormer house; the vicar is the hon. sec.

The golf clubhouse as shown on a 1904 postcard. The two storey building is the dormer house that burned down in about 1906.

159

Despite its high reputation, the course was somewhat remote from London and the "dormer house" was intended to encourage members to stay overnight. In about 1908 it burnt down and was not replaced. Membership never reached 200, settling at around 140, and the club ran at a loss which was made up by friends. Few local people would have been wealthy enough to belong to the club but they were allowed to play the course in the evenings if it was not in use.

It was taken for granted that royal occasions would be celebrated. In 1897 there was a public dinner for Queen Victoria's diamond jubilee and, in 1902, for the Coronation of Edward VII, a "public collation" for all parishioners was provided on the Lower Recreation Ground. The most elaborate celebration was for the coronation of George V in 1911. Ralph Bury, then High Sheriff of Essex, told a crowded public meeting that he was sure "that every individual parish in the county would wish to give outward expression to its loyalty in some form or other next June"; he was elected chairman of the organising committee. After a special service conducted by Thomas Goddard, the festivities took place on the Riddens. The adults enjoyed a substantial dinner and then the children assembled at the school, where the national anthem was sung and Anna Bury, Ralph's mother, presented coronation mugs. Led by the Nazeing Brass Band, the children marched to the tent for tea. Sports and dancing for adults and children followed.

"A young man of great energy" – Ralph Bury around the time he became High Sheriff of Essex.

Inevitably most informal leisure activities in any

generation go unrecorded. We are fortunate, therefore, that in the course of writing a book entitled *Romantic Essex* Alfred Beckett visited Nazeing Common in about 1900 and left the following graphic account.

...The day I first went there happened to be Whit-Monday, and a "fair" was being held in a field attached to a tavern. A woman stood ringing a large bell, after the fashion of a railway porter at a country station, outside a long barn with tarred wooden walls and a thatched roof. Expecting to find some sort of entertainment going on, I looked in, and was not disappointed. The barn was full of villagers sitting round rough tables supported by trestles and laden with goodly joints and pyramids of steaming vegetables; and before the bell had ceased ringing everyone was in place and the knives and forks in full activity. It was a club dinner, and obviously a great function. All present seemed in high good humour. I caught one sample of rustic wit. "Here, have a bit of this. It's no good waiting until it's all gone, and then saying, I should have liked a bit of that." The dialect was Essex, not Wessex; but somehow I was reminded of Mr Thomas Hardy's peasants...

The context suggests that the tavern was the Sun, although the King Harold's Head, the Black Swan, and the Lion and Lamb were also open for custom. Local pubs had always brewed their own beer. This is shown in the case of Belchers Lane next to the King Harold's Head which was formerly called Brewery Lane. Then, towards the end of the nineteenth

The Sun Inn, Nazeing Common, Essex.

The Sun at the turn of the century. It was probably the scene of the Whit-Monday fair recorded by Alfred Beckett.

century some pubs were being taken over by major brewers. The Lion and Lamb was closed by the brewers in exchange for the granting of a far more lucrative licence in the rapidly expanding suburbs of south-west Essex.

Despite his title there is no reason to doubt the basic accuracy of Beckett's account, which records vividly a way of life that was soon to pass away. That distinctive Essex dialect, for example, is little heard in the village nowadays but we can get some idea of what it sounded like. William Hone in 1638 used the Essex dialect word "wholve" to describe a culvert made from a hollowed out tree-trunk and the same word was used by a witness in the Standingford v Palmer case exactly 200 years later. There are clues to pronunciation in the accounts of the Churchwardens and Overseers of the Poor records, often written by farmers and others who were literate but lacked a high level of formal education. Apparent spelling errors may be no more than that, indicating that the writers recorded words exactly as they heard them: "armous house" (almshouse), "Bocock good" (Bocock's goods), "disburstments" (disbursements), "funell" (funeral), "sroud" (shroud), "gound" (gown), "affy davy" (affidavit), oyland and osurground (island). Peter Brent recalls that in his youth some of the older inhabitants, a few of whom may even have been at the Whitsun dinner recorded by Beckett, spoke a language rich with "thee" and "thou".

Education

Education provision in England had steadily improved during the nineteenth century but W.E. Forster's Act of 1870 was intended to make it universal. In 1875, with nonconformist support, a Nazeing School Board was established, and two years later a new Board School was built at Bumbles Green. The church school in Betts Lane, already inadequate by 1870, then closed down, only to be reopened by the vicar in 1890 to provide places for children from Broadley Common. Voluntary contributions enabled the church school to be enlarged and a government grant was obtained despite opposition from the school board, which was probably dominated by the Chapel. Most children would have been educated until the age of twelve, which was the official school leaving age. Education was now universal in theory but perhaps not in practice: in 1896, for example, George Smith of Colemans Lane was fined 5s for not sending his child to school regularly.

Bumbles Green Board School was opened in 1877 and served the village until 1958, when it was replaced by Nazeing County Primary School at Hyde Mead.

As a result of the 1902 Education Act the board school became a publicly funded "provided school" with Joseph Pegrum and Ralph Bury as its governors, while the church school became "non-provided" and privately funded. At that time both schools had 90 to 100 pupils but gradually numbers at Bumbles Green increased while those at Betts Lane decreased. In 1911 the possibility was floated of closing the church school and building a new one nearer Broxbourne. As it could have cost the parish up to £3000, the feeling was that it should be paid for out of government or county funds. These were not forthcoming, so the idea was soon dropped, not to be revived for nearly half a century. Schooling remained very much a parish matter. In 1916 a discussion at the Annual Parish Meeting resolved that a proposal for "the compulsory taking of boys from the Schools in a vehicle to learn special crafts [was] not advantageous to the education of elementary School boys and very injurious to the dicipline [sic] of both Schools".

Parish, district, and county

Towards the end of the nineteenth century the extension of the franchise to agricultural labourers and the creation of elected county, district, and parish councils undermined the power of the landed elite and took away most of the powers of the old vestries. In 1888 county councils took on the administrative responsibilities of JPs such as Ralph Palmer and Charles Bury, although their judicial role as magistrates remained intact. Then in 1894 powerful rural district councils provided an intermediate level of organisation which opened up possibilities of election to a modest level of political power to a much wider range of people and left the new secular parish councils with very limited responsibilities. The minute books of Nazeing Parish Council and other sources show that these changes, which might have been thought to affect only a small minority, contributed significantly to the emergence of the village from its long isolation and thus had a major effect on the lives of ordinary people.

Such was the tradition of deference that in many places the new councils looked little different from the old benches. In Nazeing, however, the new men seem to have made their presence felt immediately. The procedure was to elect councillors by a show of hands and at the inaugural meeting Ralph Palmer and Charles Bury withdrew their candidatures in order to avoid a poll. Of the seven elected unopposed only Reverend Thomas Goddard could be regarded as a traditional establishment figure. Joseph Pegrum was joined by four other farmers, two of whom belonged to the Chapel, and by John Banks, barrister's clerk, also a Chapel member. Perhaps in order to enable members of the establishment to continue in authority without descending to the hustings, the new parish councils were allowed to co-opt as chairman anyone qualified to be a councillor. The seven elected members chose Ralph Palmer, who in his usual business-like manner closed the first Annual Parish Meeting after five minutes with the laconic note "nothing done".

An early decision of the parish council was that its notices should be posted on the door of the chapel as well as of the church, a small but significant pointer to the nonconformist influence on the council which, in a dispute over the pay of the parish clerk, apparently divided on sectarian lines. Palmer, Goddard, and their fellow-Anglican Harry Bugg wanted to pay him £35 but the Chapel men preferred £28 and won the vote by four to three. Palmer then stated that he could not "concur in or carry out" the resolution and resigned. It is doubtful whether the other councillors expected or intended this outcome because they wrote a letter regretting Palmer's decision and thanking him for his contribution.

Perhaps demonstrating that they were not yet entirely confident in their own abilities, the councillors rather surprisingly co-opted as chairman Ernest Jerrard Wills of Snowes, a gentleman who did not otherwise make nearly as great an impression on the village as some of them. Goddard and Bugg moved a motion that

> considering we cooptated [sic] the chairman and lost his services because he could not agree to our proceedings and bearing in mind we are not a representative Council however good a Council we may be we elect a Chairman from our own body rather than cooptating a chairman from outside.

They lost the vote by five to two. Wills's chairmanship was apparently

The immaculate copperplate writing of George Lipson who recorded the affairs of the parish council and the chapel for over twenty years.

less forceful than Palmer's. Anyone who has taken minutes can sympathise with the clerk's record of a debate in 1898: "A general discussion upon the subject took place, but nothing of a definite character was resolved upon." Evidently any bad feelings did not persist because in 1901 Palmer was elected by the voters as a parish councillor and then by his colleagues as chairman, a position which he held, with Joseph Pegrum as his vice-chairman, until he stood down twenty years later at the age of 81. Ironically, the chapel secretary, George Lipson, was appointed clerk shortly after the disagreement. By 1904 his salary had been raised to £36 10s, although this did include additional duties.

In many villages such events would have heralded the quiet retreat of the old gentry but in Nazeing this did not happen. By 1914 indeed they had recovered much of their former authority. The new councillors had the perfect opportunity to take power but they were not social or political radicals and preferred to share it. Joseph Pegrum, for example, was the district councillor but only after Charles Bury had died and again when Ralph Bury had stood down. Pegrum was an exceptionally capable individual but nobody else of his type emerged with similar influence. In 1921 Archdale Palmer replaced his uncle as chairman of the parish council, though he had never even been a member before. Only after the Second World War, when Archdale Palmer and Ralph Bury had died without male heirs, did the old pattern of village leadership finally disappear.

Allotments and Recreation Grounds

The parish council still controlled some matters, such as the allocation and management of allotments, which required local knowledge but comparatively little expenditure. For most villagers growing their own produce was both a leisure activity and an important source of food. They grew their own vegetables, bottled their own fruit, made their own jam, and kept chickens and rabbits. The parish council took its responsibilities in this area very seriously and in 1895 provided prizes of 15s, 10s, 6s, and 4s for the best cottage gardens, although it is unclear whether this experiment was not repeated or simply not recorded again.

As part of an attack on the great landowners the new reforming Liberal government brought in the Small Holdings and Allotments Act of 1907, designed to release underused land to labourers. On 20th March 1908 the parish council issued notices inviting applications for allotments and at the Annual Parish Meeting the following day Ralph Palmer made a lengthy statement on the provisions of the Act.   The parish council

NAZEING PARISH COUNCIL.

Small Holdings and Allotments Act, 1907.

The following applications for allotments have been received by the Council, in reply to Notices issued on the 20th March last:—

Name.	Residence.	Application.	Employment.
Walter Samuel.	" Upper Town."	4 acres of land.	Independent.
Thomas Webb.	Do.	4 or 5 acres of land.	Do.
James Flack.	Do.	20 poles of allotment ground.	Gardener.
James Mansfield.	Do.	20 poles of garden ground.	Employed in Powder Mills.

The Council have duly considered the foregoing applications; and they find:—

That Walter Samuel is an independent occupier of some seven acres of land and buildings; and is not one of the labouring population referred to in the Allotments Acts.

That Thomas Webb is an occupier of a considerable quantity of land and buildings; and is in a similar position to Walter Samuel.

That James Flack is not an occupier of any tenement or land in Nazeing; and that his employment as a gardener is wholly at Waltham Abbey, at Messrs. Honor's Nursery Gardens. It is not alleged that any application by this applicant to hire a tenement or lands in Nazeing, or in Waltham Abbey, by agreement, has not received or would not receive due consideration.

That James Mansfield is in occupation of a tenement and garden in Nazeing; and has been employed in the Government Powder Mills at Waltham Abbey for some seven years past. It is not alleged that any application by this applicant for a larger holding has ever been made, or refused.

Having considered the cases of the several applicants, and their respective employments, the Council is of opinion that there exists no such unsatisfied demand for allotments by members of the labouring population in Nazeing, as would justify the intervention of external authority; and that any reasonable requirements may be left to arrangement between landlords and tenants.

The public notice explaining why the parish council disallowed all four applications for allotments. Although James Flack resided in Nazeing, he did not receive an allotment. He died in the First World War and his name is included on the memorial in All Saints'.

investigated four applications for allotments and issued a public notice explaining its reasons for disallowing them all. Thus the new measure was not an unqualified success in Nazeing

Although women did not obtain the suffrage in national elections until 1918, from 1894 they were entitled to vote in and even stand for parish council elections. It was not until 1934, however, that Nazeing elected a female parish councillor. An episode in 1911 may suggest that this reflected a general attitude towards women. Two of the allotment holders had died and their land was being maintained by the widow of one and the daughter of the other, while another holder, Edward Brace, had been convicted of assault. After some discussion it was decided to give the women notice to vacate their allotments within four months but to take no action over Brace. Later in the century this would have been seen as sexist and illegal but even then it seems to have raised eyebrows, as the clerk was asked to investigate the rules of the Board of Agriculture and reported that they "allowed any man or woman resident in the Parish and belonging to the labouring population to be tenant of an allotment".

There were two Recreation Grounds, the Upper one being the Betts Lane Triangle and the Lower where the Bumbles Green Leisure Centre is now. The Upper Ground was used as a playing field for the church school and the Lower Ground for the celebration of the coronation of Edward VII, both probably typical of the ways in which the grounds were used, although little evidence survives. A sensible arrangement enabled parishioners to tender for the right to put their stock on the grounds: this gave the parish council a small income, the farmers an extra grazing area, and the fields very effective mobile lawn mowers in the form of sheep. One early decision forbade the use of great cattle because they could be dangerous to children. In 1906, for example, Ralph Palmer offered to repair the fences and plant willows at the Upper Ground and for many years afterwards paid £1 5s a year for grazing rights. In 1914, when the tenant of the Lower Ground had complained that the gate had been broken down so that his sheep could get out, the council agreed "that something should be put on the top rail ... to prevent boys ... sitting on the gate and causing damage".

Parish pump politics

The inhabitants of Nazeing had always been largely dependent on wells for their supply of water. In 1879 a tube well was provided at

Nazeing Gate by the landowner there and in 1888 the owners of seven cottages at Reynolds Gate (at the junction of Common Road and Betts Lane) provided and paid for their own supply. The newly established rural district councils, however, were given far-reaching powers over matters of health. When in 1895 Epping RDC's sanitary inspector visited the Nazeing Gate area, he was very concerned over the quality of the water there. Complicated negotiations over the best way to remedy the situation dragged on for ten years and caused great ill feeling on all sides.

In 1896, on the proposal of John Banks, who lived at Coburg House (now Warwick House), the parish council suggested to William Graham as tenant of Harold's Park Farm the possibility of laying pipes to take the overflow from his springs to Nazeing Gate. The terms offered by Graham's landlord were deemed unsatisfactory and the negotiations were dropped. In August 1898 Banks complained to the district council that "people in the vicinity of Nazeing Gate were practically without drinking water" and "soon there will be no water for cattle as the ponds are drying up". Not long afterwards the sanitary inspector reported that there was "no water at Nazeing, and the nearest is at Waltham Abbey".

In 1899, therefore, Epping RDC installed at Reynolds Gate a pump and a notice board claiming ownership of the existing facilities. On the Common at Nazeing Gate it built a tank containing 20-25,000 gallons of water drawn from a pond in the garden of Coburg House. It informed the parish council, which reported that the inhabitants were "well satisfied both as to the quality and quantity" of the water but, with extraordinary lack of courtesy, it failed to notify the trustees of the Common or the individual owners. This would have been tactless at the best of times but, as the chairman of the trustees and owner of most of the Reynolds Gate properties happened to be Ralph Palmer, in antagonising him they aroused a formidable adversary.

In a memo to the trust's solicitors, Jessopp and Gough, Palmer attacked the "so-called waterworks" as "ousting the jurisdiction of the owners" and "a stupid waste of £200 of public money". Although a pure supply was available from Harold's Park Farm at a reasonable rental, the rural district council had chosen to install a tank "to secure the same water which the public had the easement right to dip from Mr. Banks' pond". The water was "neither pure nor wholesome nor fit for consumption", and had been condemned by the council's own Medical Officer of Health and sanitary inspector. The trust should "ask to be in a position as if the district council had proceeded by law" because "the real obstruction and objection comes from the mounters of this scheme". Palmer added that Joseph Pegrum was a member of Epping Rural District Council and of Nazeing Parish Council, as well as being a trustee of the Common. This rather mischievous observation perhaps alluded to the mixed allegiances of the man who had recently defeated Ralph's nephew in an election for trustee.

The work began in January 1900, shortly after a meeting of the parish council which was not due to meet again until April. Palmer was then in self-imposed exile from the council and, when he raised the matter at the Annual Parish Meeting, Jerrard Wills as chairman refused to allow any discussion. This can scarcely have improved Palmer's temper. Supported by Ralph Bury, he called for a Special Parish Meeting which he "addressed at great length". He complained about the quality of the water, arguing that deep wells should have been dug to fresh sources and moved a resolution that "... a tank supplied from Mr. Banks' Garden pond cannot ... constitute a supply of wholesome water ... for which the entire district or parish of Nazeing ought to be rated ..." The meeting was attended by 48 electors and the resolution was carried comfortably, with four votes against and a few abstentions. Ralph Palmer was more used to exercising authority than opposing it, so this episode was probably instrumental in his decision to stand for election to the parish council at the earliest opportunity.

The parish council seems to have retreated in some haste from its support for the tank scheme. This chastening experience may explain its vigorous opposition to ambitious and expensive new proposals put forward by the South Essex Water Board. Its case, argued in a letter to the district council, gives a vivid portrait of the village as it moved into the new century:

> The Parish is sparsely populated and very scattered and only in a few instances has any inconvenience been felt from deficient water supply ... The population is at a standstill and to put in force a general water scheme at the present time would cause for many years a very heavy expenditure to a district which is a purely agricultural one.

Nothing came of this scheme but eventually, after five years of negotiations, the Trustees of Nazeing Wood or Park granted a licence for the tank to Epping RDC, which agreed to pay their expenses. The parish council, back under the chairmanship of Ralph Palmer, completed its about face and refused to make a contribution because "the proceedings were wholly caused by error on the part of the District Council".

In the same year, 1905, came a threat from the even more powerful Metropolitan Water Board. First the board applied for permission to abstract more water from the Lea and Stort rivers, which the parish council opposed because it would increase rates and reduce water levels in Nazeing Mead and Marsh. Then the council learnt, not from the MWB but from Epping RDC, that the board had shifted the proposed location for a 150-acre sewage works from a site in Roydon to one in Nazeing, between North Street and the church. There were only ten days to the closing date for objections, so the parish council rapidly convened a public meeting at which 46 inhabitants voted unanimously to oppose the scheme. Ralph Palmer, who was the Nazeing delegate in a deputation from the affected local councils which negotiated with the MWB, declared that the parish "objected to paying for something from which it received no benefit". Joseph Pegrum proposed a resolution which the parish council carried unanimously, recording

> their hearty thanks to the Chairman R.C. Palmer Esqu. for the great assistance financially and otherwise he so kindly and expeditiously rendered the Parishioners in preventing the then proposed Sewage Works from being brought into the Parish.

In 1907 the parish council was successful in opposing an attempt by the Herts and Essex Waterworks Company to begin operations in Nazeing but in the following year the council's response to a new plan was more equivocal. Over the next few years the company began to extend its service to various parts of the village and by 1912 it wanted to lay pipes along Middle Street. The parish council declined to contribute because the houses were too isolated but Joseph Pegrum negotiated an arrangement whereby the owners there paid a total of £120 and the installation went ahead.

"An improvement for the solitary parish of Nazeing"

Not all of the parish council's campaigns were negative: it played a vital part in the creation of a new road to Broxbourne. The idea was first mooted in 1895, when Reverend Thomas Goddard proposed that the parish should "memorialize" the district and county councils to "promote free access by road between the counties of Essex & Herts at Broxbourne Station", which was the nearest to Nazeing and an important junction. The only route across the Lea, used by over seventy vehicles a day, was the narrow private road and bridge near the Crown, for which a heavy toll was charged. Many Nazeing people used stations at the next-nearest river crossing points, Waltham Cross and Roydon, respectively six and four miles away, rather than negotiate the dangerous level crossing at Broxbourne.

The inevitable council committee was set up and later in the year made its recommendations. A new road should be constructed across a meadow belonging to Ralph Palmer and a marsh owned by George Smith-Bosanquet of Broxbourne, thus shortening the distance to Broxbourne station by 600 yards and avoiding the level crossing. It was impossible to calculate actual costs, but the benefits would justify the levying of a special rate.

It was to be another twelve years before the road was built. In 1899 Epping RDC agreed to ask Essex County Council to put £2,000 into the scheme provided that Nazeing Parish Council matched its proposed contribution of £500; this course was agreed upon. The work was to be done in conjunction with Hertfordshire and, when a district councillor suggested that it had got the best of the bargain, Joseph Pegrum replied that Hertfordshire had been "very liberal". The Great Eastern Railway, which was to "spend £17,000 towards opening up Nazeing", wined and dined councillors at the sumptuous Liverpool Street Hotel and obtained their support for a private Act of Parliament which included construction of bridges for the new road. Questions were regularly asked at parish meetings as to the progress of the scheme but it remained "in abeyance" until 1905, when the GER promoted a new bill which sought "to destroy the agreement entered into in 1899". The county and district councils, urged by the parish council, successfully opposed the bill. This was the catalyst for matters to move much more quickly. In 1907 a tender for £11,301 6s 4d was accepted and Hertfordshire, Essex, and Epping Councils agreed to share the costs.

There have been various explanations for the curious layout of the bridge by the station. It may have been necessitated by the geology of the area and the need to find firm gravel footings for the pillars. Originally there were plans for the railway to be broadened to four tracks, which the wider bridge would have accommodated. There is also a possibility that one of the local landowners applied pressure on the builders to provide a private track across his ballast pits to the river at Carthagena Lock. Further research may provide an answer to this puzzle.

A newspaper reported that the two county councils had agreed to pay £100 to each of the owners of "the Tatsford's Estate" as compensation for the road's crossing their land. This prompted a letter from Jerrard Wills, the former parish council chairman, who had moved to Moreton, near Ongar. He regretted that "local landowners have not responded more generously" and claimed that, although the road would give additional access between Essex and Herts, it would be "first and foremost an improvement for the solitary parish of Nazeing". He continued: "So far as the parishioners are concerned, it will save them the inconvenience of waiting at the railway level crossing and *chiefly* it will save their pockets from the present toll road." Improved access to the "almost unrivalled train service" would result in a great rise in land values so that "landlord and tenant in this favoured spot would rejoice together"; Essex County Council should therefore make a repayable loan rather than a grant.

There may be an element of sour grapes here. When Ralph Palmer had returned to the parish council in 1901, Wills had been dropped unceremoniously, without even a vote of thanks for his six years of service, so perhaps he was attempting to get his own back. If so, he succeeded. Palmer had only just put some of his own money into the successful fight against the sewage scheme and, apparently, agreed to forgo his compensation. Alexander Frogley, who owned the land where his sons later ran Broxbourne Aerodrome, was less accommodating, so Ralph Bury and "two other gentlemen" guaranteed £300 towards expenses. Nazeing Parish Council contributed an additional £70 so that the road could go across Tatsford rather than follow a less direct route, roughly along the line of present day Green Lane and Riverside Avenue. They levied a 3d rate which produced £55 and a special Overseers' precept for the remaining £15, transactions which aroused the interest of the Auditor. The sense of the minutes is somewhat unclear but it would appear that the means used to raise the £15 were deemed illegal so that the councillors were surcharged personally for it.

Whatever Wills's motives, there was much truth in his comments. The new road, "thrown open to the public" in January 1909, had its problems. For example, Walter Hargreaves complained that his maid had suffered an accident because Hertfordshire had not repaired its section. Nevertheless it was the development which, perhaps more than any other, ended the feeling that Nazeing was "five miles from everywhere". Whereas there had been access to Hertfordshire and the railway only via an expensive toll road and a dangerous level crossing, suddenly it was easy to get to both. Nazeing was no longer on the edge of west Essex but at the heart of the Lea Valley.

Roads and footpaths

There were few changes to the parish road network in the nineteenth century. Paynes Lane rather than Colemans Lane became the main access to Langridge, and Nursery Road was built to link Sedge Green and Nazeing Road.

Flooding was a perennial problem for which the parish council will not have been sorry to lose responsibility. George Crow was the owner of Maple Croft, known, by a rather neat pun on its elevated position and his name, as The Crow's Nest. In 1880 he wrote to the vestry to complain that the right of way to his house was "quite impassable" and added that he had "been trying for years to get the Lane made so as to enable me to get to and from the house with horse and Cart". Ralph Palmer had "offered to give as many loads of Gravel as the Parish towards the repair of the Lane" but nothing had been done, so Crow could neither live there nor let the property. Advised that the parish had a duty to keep the road in good repair, he threatened that "the necessary proceedings will be taken on my part to compel it". Evidently the problem remained unresolved

The ford through Nazeing Brook in Middle Street. At this point it used to be known as Deans Brook, from the family which had farmed at Burnt Hall and Brook House. The brook flooded Middle Street on several occasions well into the twentieth century. Wheelers is in the centre of the picture.

because, fifteen years later, Crow brought it to the parish council, which advised him to "appeal to the Surveyor or to the District Council".

In a similar episode in 1891 Nazeing Brook caused major flooding at Greenleaves, Mansion House Farm, the pound at the crossroads, and Marshgate Farm. The only course of action was to bank and pipe the brook but the vestry was divided over the cost, although it did agree to widen the brook at Greenleaves. In 1904 serious flooding at Deans Brook made the road dangerous and the parish reported it to the district, which in turn asked the parish how much it intended to contribute to the proposed remedial work. In a distinctly waspish reply which perhaps reveals the considerable legal expertise in its ranks, the parish council stated that "they hardly considered it their duty to make suggestions as to how the cost should be met otherwise than as directed by Parliament". Joseph Pegrum met district officials and reported that "they were obtaining an Estimate as to the probable Cost of a suitable bridge". Evidently the expense would have been too great and nothing was done because in 1919 one of the suggestions for an appropriate war memorial was the provision of a bridge at Deans Brook.

The parish council often attempted to resolve problems about footpaths, stiles, and bridges, either by direct action or by negotiation. For some reason there was a rash of complaints in 1912 and 1913; in each case Ralph Palmer as chairman visited the site. Thomas Goddard complained repeatedly about the condition of footpaths leading to the church, so the parish council asked James Pegrum to clear out a ditch and "Messrs. Palmer and Lawrence [did] what they could to improve the footpath". The minutes then record rather testily that "everything possible has been done to drain away the water from the approaches to the footpaths and it was not possible to do anything further". A bridge at Damsel Mead, near Rusheymead, was reported as being in a dangerous condition and Palmer recommended that it should be rebuilt. The owners did nothing, however, so the parish council did the work and the expenses "fell upon the Rates instead of upon the Owners". The footpath alongside the Sun became impassable and Palmer found that the fence around the nearby pond had broken down. The owners, by contrast with those at Damsel Mead, repaired the fence and regravelled the path immediately, for which prompt action the parish council wrote to thank them. It may have been as a result of these problems that Joseph Pegrum "got a resolution passed at the Rural District Council ... directing that each Parish was to bear the cost of upkeeping its own footpaths".

The railway is the obvious means by which Nazeing was drawn into the wider world but not to be overlooked is the humble bicycle, invented in the 1880s. By 1900 organised cycling clubs and more informal groups were exploring the countryside around London. Some older Londoners recall the joys of puffing up the hill over the Common. Nazeing people also obtained bicycles and soon used them to go further afield, although they often suffered punctures on the gravel roads, which in summer were dusty and in winter muddy, with six-inch potholes. One man saved up for a bicycle so that he could ride to his work at the Waltham Abbey Gunpowder Factory, only to have it stolen on the first day he used it.

In 1896 the traction engine and trucks of the Roydon Brickfield Company were regularly passing through Nazeing. The parish council saw them as "a great nuisance to many persons having charge of horses and carts and other Vehicles" and the roads and bridges over which they passed as "totally unfit for such dangerous and extraordinary traffic". The parish asked Essex County Council not to grant the company a licence for the engine and trucks; since there is no further reference to the problem, presumably the request was successful.

The twentieth century has been described as "the age of the motorcar", so it is appropriate that the first mention of the car at Epping Rural District Council was at its first meeting of the century. The issue came up again in 1903, when there was a motion to restrict speeds to twenty miles per hour. Ralph Bury, who was one of the first people in Nazeing to own a car and in *Who's Who* listed one of his recreations as motoring, said: "I think cars might go at any speed on a straight wide road with no one about". "Ah, but what if there *is* someone about?" commented the chairman, and the motion was carried by nine to four.

The Nazeing pig

In 1901 there began an improbable saga which would be dismissed as a folk myth, if it were not so well documented. Epping Rural District Council used its new powers to summon George Hampton and his daughter Emily to the Epping Petty Sessions for "keeping a pig in a manner injurious to the health of the public". The council's sanitary inspector and medical officer visited the cottage, near the Bumbles Green Board School, where they found an enormous pig called Totty. It was lying comfortably between clean sheets on a nine foot featherbed covered with a lace counterpane and with its head on a pillow. Its room was furnished like a parlour, with scripture texts on the wall and a notice in the window saying "Sixpence to see this pig". Despite bursts of rather unkind laughter, Emily Hampton gave her evidence in a strikingly earnest manner which displayed great affection for her pet. She stated that she made no secret of the pig, which in the past four years had been visited by people from near and far. She lulled it to sleep like a baby and washed its bedclothes twice a week. It was a well-educated pig and always asked to go out when it wanted to. It dined with the family, was treated as one of them, and "behaved in many respects like a Christian".

The magistrates adjourned the case to give the Hamptons time to build a pigsty well away from the house but six weeks later nothing had happened. Emily had consulted a surveyor named Rawlings but, "owing to the inclemency of the weather and the remoteness of the spot", he had been unable to visit. The bench gave the defendants another six weeks, after which they would pay 10s a day until a place for the pig was complete. George Hampton duly built a house for the pig but "the animal

Emily Hampton with her mother at the grave of her beloved pet pig, the forty stone Totty. A picture of Emily and Totty is on the jacket.

refused to inhabit it and had returned to the house", so a council official was instructed to take proceedings.

Apparently the Hamptons complied because nothing further is recorded for another seven years. Then, after the council had written to her again, her reply was read out at a council meeting. She had been unwell and the cottage had become so dilapidated that the family had been living in the pig's room for three years, so her letter makes sad reading:

> I received your letter this morning, and I felt very much cut up ... as to get rid of him off the premises, I shall do no such thing as he is no nuisance to anyone and goes to the orchard twice a day ... I am not going to get rid of my pet; we must all live together. I will move him as soon as God gives me the strength to do so.

The Reverend T.C. Spurgin remarked that "the lady would require a good deal of strength to move her pet", which weighed 40 stone; the matter was referred to the Sanitary Committee for consideration.

There is a remarkable epilogue to the story. By 1930 the cottage was literally falling down and, although Emily Hampton was still living there, together with a large number of animals, it was declared unfit for habitation. Epping RDC obtained a possession order to demolish the cottage and it was replaced by a pair of semi-detached cottages, one occupied by the Hamptons and one by Andrew and Louie Welch. When Andrew dug over his new garden, he unearthed some of the pig's bones and the Hamptons insisted on having them for reburial. Emily had commissioned a cross for the pig from a Broadley Common funeral director, who later sold his premises where, in the late 1990s, Peter Lewis came upon the original cross.

CHAPTER 8

NAZEING JUST BEFORE THE GREAT WAR

As late as 1907 Edward Hardingham thought fit to quote that Nazeing "lies high and dry and five miles from everywhere." In many ways during the years just before the Great War it would have been more familiar to its inhabitants of six centuries earlier than to its inhabitants today. Ralph Charlton Palmer owned much land and many houses in the north of the village and Ralph Bury had a fair sized holding at the southern end. Both having considerable local influence, the squirearchy might not have been thought so different from the mediaeval lords of the manor. The population in 1900 was 795, only a third as big again as in 1300, and, just as then, the majority of workers were engaged in farming or related activities.

Nazeing Wood or Park was rough grazing, not wholly unlike its use in the days of Waltham Abbey, and farms in Nazeing, as in most of England, were mixed, with dairy cows, pigs, sheep, and arable. The freeholders and copyholders still had rights of pasturage on Nazeing Marsh and the privilege of fishing in the Lea. The first glass houses were not to arrive until about 1920, so that the view westwards from the church overlooked "mile upon mile of fertile land." The bells of All Saints' could be heard clearly in Hoddesdon, where lived Alfred Manser. When he died in 1903, he left £300 to the church as a generous mark of appreciation.

Visitors seem to have been struck by the trees in the village, which helped to give an impression of picturesque seclusion, with "the tree-shaded churchyard", entered by a stile, chestnut trees, as now, at the churchyard gate, and a beautiful avenue of poplars along the road running eastwards from the Crown. There were also forest trees, which one, less poetic, writer noted looked very bad and sickly because of continually recurring droughts.

There had been a few minor changes to the pattern of roads: the Palmers and the Burys had re-routed roads away from their respective front doors, some tracks had fallen into disuse, and others had gained in importance. Wholesale additions to the road system did not start for another quarter century and their surfaces were not to be tarmac until the 1920s. The only utility which had come to the village, and that just to some parts, was water. There was no gas, electricity, main drainage, or telephone.

What might have impressed a visitor from Edward I's time the most was the improvement in housing. Even discounting the grand mansions, the average dwelling, though lacking our accepted conveniences, was vastly more comfortable than a mediaeval cottage. The houses were described as being of wood, with thatched roofs, gable ends, and low eaves, and often massive chimney-stacks outside the main building. Nevertheless the district was said to be badly off for smaller houses, although the size of the population had hardly changed for fifty years.

Such a visitor, with his keen eye for farming practices, would have noted also, within the basic mixed farming pattern, enormous changes. The modern system of rotation of crops had brought about a much more efficient use of the land. Cattle, like Palmer's "beautiful" Herefords, gave an air of prosperity. His reliance on large dressings of farmyard muck, which received Rider Haggard's approval, was a practice unchanged from before the Middle Ages but Bury's experimentation with different combinations of artificial fertiliser to see which produced the best hay foreshadowed future methods. Hay was the most important crop to Nazeing; other crops grown were wheat and barley, root crops, including particularly potatoes, and beans.

The Coach and Horses, the first view of Nazeing from the south.

180

There were twenty-two farmers in Nazeing, apart from the gentry. Joseph Pegrum of Nazeing Bury, holding 600 acres, of which 200 were arable, was one of the most substantial. Industry was no more than trades with a local market, blacksmith, wheelwright, carpenter, builder, and shoemaker. Apart from these tradesmen there were four shopkeepers and a general dealer in the village. The shoemaker and one shopkeeper were also subpostmasters and the pillar letter box at Greenleaves was cleared daily.

The public houses mentioned in Kelly's Directories at the time were The Sun, The Red Lion (now the White House in Middle Street), The Crooked Billet, The Coach and Horses, and The Crown. This last, standing at the end of the bridge from Broxbourne, was on the road between Nazeing and Broxbourne until Nazeing New Road was built in 1908. It was described as a pretty little hostelry, beside an angler's paradise. There had been at least one other pub in Nazeing, the Lion and Lamb, by Harknett's Gate, as well as two pubs apart from the Black Swan in Broadley Common. One of those was called the Hop Poles.

Nazeing was only a moderately prosperous village at this time. Agricultural wage rates were poor, even if not quite as low as the average for Essex, Suffolk, and Norfolk, which was the lowest in the country. The advent of the railways had removed Essex's advantage of proximity to London, though Nazeing's being within fairly easy carting distance compared with the north and east of the county must have had some beneficial effect on incomes. Nevertheless, the many years around the turn of the century when agricultural prices were depressed brought considerable anxiety to the village.

Nazeing's almost complete dependence on farming was soon to end. Although we may look on the First World War as a watershed, change would have come anyway, perhaps even more quickly without the huge expenditure of money and lives which the two wars brought about. The coming of the railway to Broxbourne had not affected Nazeing greatly; improvements to road transport and the arrival of utilities in the twenties and thirties, however, meant that the village would become an attractive place to live for those who earned modest incomes outside the immediate area. The 1920s were to mark the end of a long era and the beginning of a new one which requires a volume to itself.

Archdale Palmer who came to play a leading role in Nazeing after 1920.

GLOSSARY

Admittance fine   A feudal due paid to the lord on being admitted to a tenancy. It continued to be paid by copyholders on admission. (A bit like Stamp Duty today.)

Advowson   The right to present to an ecclesiastical benefice; therefore in Nazeing the right to appoint the vicar.

Amercement   A fine paid in a manorial court. The tenant was said to be "in mercy" of the court.

Augustinian canons   Known as "Austin", "Black", or "Regular" Canons. They resided in communities, following the Rule of St. Augustine of Hippo (354-430).

Beanfeast   An annual dinner for employees in the nineteenth century. The name seems to be derived from the practice of serving bacon and beans.

Belgic   Tribes in the second Celtic invasion of Britain, just before 100 B.C.

The Black Death   Bubonic plague, spread across Europe by black rats. It reached Sicily first, in November 1347, and England a year later. The first outbreak, which was devasting, was followed by several more that century and sporadic ones later. The last notable outbreak in England was in 1665.

Bordars   On a mediaeval manor they had less land than villeins, probably towards the edge of the village.

Churchwardens   An office recognised legally by the thirteenth century and subject to annual election two hundred years later, making it the oldest elective office in England. Local governmental powers were given to them from *c.*1550 until 1894. Now their powers relate to ecclesiastical matters only.

The Civil War   From 1642 to 1646 and in 1648, between King Charles I and Parliament.

Coppicing   The practice of cutting down mature trees to ground level to induce new growth, whence copse, coppice, and, in Nazeing, Copy Wood.

Copyhold tenure   Tenure by copy of the manor court roll. It developed from villein tenure to become a form of ownership registered locally.

Court Baron   (*Curia baronis*) A court kept by the lord of the manor for his freehold tenants to enforce the customs of the manor in property matters. The freemen were bound to attend and, with the lord, were the judges.

Court Customary   A manor court for the tenants in villeinage to deal with property matters according to the customs of the manor. The lord's steward was the only judge. When tenure in villeinage had evolved into copyhold, all property matters came to the courts baron.

Court Leet   A court in private hands with jurisdiction in tort, contract, and petty crime. Most manors had such a court but in some places the older vill or township court exercised such jurisdiction.

Custumal   A document so called because it summarised the customs of the manor.

Delinquent   A name for those who assisted Charles I or Charles II in levying war, 1642 - 1660.

Demesne   Reserved for a feudal lord's use, a home farm.

Escheat   A feudal lord's right to ownerless real property.

Estover   Wood which a tenant may take from the land.

Freehold tenure   In the Middle Ages tenure free of feudal obligations; since the abolition of copyhold tenure the normal holding of real property.

Hearth Tax   Levied at 2s. per hearth on the houses of the better off from 1662 until repealed in 1689 owing to its unpopularity.

Honour   A grouping of several knight's fees, lordships, or manors.

Hundred   Administrative division of a shire, probably established in the tenth century; existed formally until 1894.

Induct   To introduce formally to an ecclesiastical benefice or living.

The Iron Age   The prehistoric period when iron came to be used for tools and weapons, in Europe following the Bronze Age. In Britain it lasted from about 500B.C. until 43A.D.

Jury   As in manorial jury, a group summoned because of their knowledge of an area and its customs and happenings. They were sworn in to give evidence and to witness the court's proceedings. This type of jury originated in the ninth century and continues in the U.S.A. as the grand jury. The petty jury, summoned to decide disputes on evidence presented to it, came into existence in the thirteenth century.

Knights Hospitaller   In full, Knights of the Order of the Hospital of St. John of Jerusalem.   The order was founded in the eleventh century and became prominent and wealthy during the Crusades. Its property in England was sequestrated in 1540. It was revived in 1831 on a mainly Anglican basis and was responsible for founding the St. John's Ambulance.

Lay Subsidy   A system of taxing personal property introduced in 1181, the so-called Saladin Tithe. Later it was paid by laymen only and was extended to rents and wages. It was assessed by royal collectors and was collected last in 1623.

Manor   A territorial and jurisdictional holding.

Manor courts   There were two courts which were the outcome of tenure, the Court Baron and the Court Customary. A manor could have in addition a Court Leet, which had assumed the powers of other courts, particularly those of the vill and the hundred. All the courts followed local customs.

Marl   Decayed chalky soil used for fertilizer, often used by agricultural improvers in the seventeenth century.

Mesolithic   Relating to the Middle Stone Age, which lasted in England from *c.*8000 to *c.*3700B.C.

Nazeing Park   Developed by William Palmer from Lucas Hill Farm. Although it is contiguous with Nazeing Wood or Park, none of it was ever part of the area emparked by Abbot and Canons of Waltham.

Nazeing Wood or Park   This is the official name for what is known otherwise as Nazeingwood Common or, in Nazeing, as just "The Common". Strictly it is not a common; as far as we know, the tenure is unique. It is the remainder of the area emparked by the Abbot and Canons of Waltham in 1225.

Neolithic   Relating to the New Stone Age, which lasted in England from *c.*3700 to *c.*1700B.C.

Pinder   Spelt pindar in Nazeing. Officer in charge of a pound, into which stray animals were put.

The Poor Law   Attempts to control vagrancy were made from 1388. Poor Law Acts were passed from 1563. Overseers of the Poor, elected by each vestry, became compulsory under the Poor Law Relief Act 1601. They collected the poor rate which was used to put paupers to work. In 1723 small parishes were empowered to set up workhouses. The provision of "Outdoor Relief" was minimised in 1834, when confinement in a workhouse was made the central element of the system. The last parts of the Poor Law were repealed in 1929.

Queen Anne's Bounty   A fund established in 1704 to receive from Anne ecclesiastical dues which had been annexed by Henry VIII. The fund was used for the benefit of poor clergy. In 1948 it became part of the Church Commission.

Quit rent   Payment made by tenants to excuse themselves from manor services.

Quitclaim   Release.

Rector   A priest who had the right to the tithes of an ecclesiastical benefice. When a monastery acquired the rights of a rectory it appointed a vicar to take the services in its stead. The titles came to point only to a historical difference.

Reversion   What a tenant in fee simple (usually called the owner nowadays) retains after granting a life interest or a lease for a term of years.

Secular canons   Clergy bound by a life together but who went out among the people. Regular canons were in a community under a rule which governed their daily life in an institution.

Seisin   The possession of land by a freeholder.

Sequestration   Taking over by higher authorities, in particular county committees, which collected rents and fines, and assigned leases.

Serfs   Those on a mediaeval manor with practically no land.

The Vestry   Organisation of local government based on the ecclesiastical parish to which were delegated various powers by legislation from the later sixteenth century onwards.   It was usually narrowed to a select group of well-to-do parishioners.

Villeins   Literally those serving at a *villa*, and so those holding land in a village, whose feudal due was to work for the lord of the manor for set days a week, and extra at harvest, and so on.

Waltham Abbey   The church in the village of Waltham became the church of an Augustinian priory in 1177. The priory became an abbey in 1184. The abbey exists no longer but the name persists for the town.

Waste   Land on a manor not arable, meadow, or wood. Some of it was beside roads; it provided casual grazing for pigs, geese, and other animals.

CURRENCY, WEIGHTS, AND MEASURES

Currency   £.s.d, *libri, solidi, denarii*, Roman names for their coins adopted for English pounds, shillings, and pence. 12 pence = 1 shilling, 20 shillings = 1 pound, 21 shillings = 1 guinea.

Weights   14 pounds (lbs) = 1 stone, 8 stones = 1 hundredweight (cwt., about 51 kilograms), 20 cwt. = 1 ton.

Capacity   1 gallon (about 4½ litres) is the volume of water which weighs 10 lbs. 2 gallons = 1 peck, 4 pecks = 1 bushel.

Distance   The basic surveyor's measure, called a rod, pole, or perch, was a stick 5½ yards (about 5 metres) long. 4 rods = 1 chain, 10 chains = 1 furlong, 8 furlongs = 1 mile.

Area   1 acre is 1 furlong by 1 chain and is therefore 4,840 square yards (about $^2/_5$ of a hectare); 640 acres = 1 square mile.

BIBLIOGRAPHY

Five miles from everywhere is based on a wide range of primary and secondary sources but, in order to save space and keep down costs, there are no footnotes in the book. A longer, fully sourced version of the text is available on application to Nazeing History Workshop, or for reference at Essex Record Office. Copies of extracts from *Nazeing Parish Magazine* and *Nazeing Parish News* and a copy of *Palmer of Nazing* have been deposited with these papers. Other items should be available through the public library service but, in case of difficulty, please contact Nazeing History Workshop c/o Colin Dauris, Goodalls, Middle Street, Nazeing, Essex EN9 2LP.

The following are the sources of which most use has been made:

Printed books and articles

ADDISON, William. Portrait of Epping Forest. London, Hale 1977.

ANGEL, J.L. Mead of memories: a record of the graves in the old churchyard of All Saints' Nazeing in the county of Essex. Nazeing Conservation Society, 1985.

BASCOMBE, K.N. Two Charters of King Suebred of Essex. in NEALE, K. (ed.) *An Essex Tribute*, 1987.

BONNETT, Norman and HUTCHINGS, Paddy. Nonconformity in Nazeing: a history of the Congregational Church. Nazeing, P.Hutchings, [1999].

BROWN, A.F.J. Prosperity and poverty: rural Essex 1700-1815. Chelmsford, Essex Record Office, 1996.

CHARLESWORTH, Andrew (ed). An atlas of rural protest in Britain, 1548-1900. London, Croom Helm, 1983.

COLLER, D.W. People's history of Essex. 1861.

DAURIS, Colin. All Saints Church Nazeing: a short history and guide. 1997.

DICTIONARY of National Biography.

EMMISON, F.G. Elizabethan wills of South-west Essex. Waddesdon, Kylin Press, 1983.

FISHER, John L. The Deanery of Harlow. Colchester, Benham, 1922.

FISHER, W.R. The Forest of Essex. 1887.

GERVIS, John H. Nazeing Bury: the story of a house and its people. Nazeing Books, 1997.

GELLING, Margaret. Place-names in the landscape: the geographical roots of Britain's place-names. London, Dent, 1984.

GIBBONS, C. Nazeing's heritage buildings. Nazeing Conservation Society, 1987.

HAGGARD, H. Rider. Rural England. London, Longman, 1902.

HARDINGHAM, Edward. Lays and legends of the forest of Essex. London, 1907.

HILL, Christopher. The century of revolution 1603-1714, 2nd ed. London, Routledge, 1980.

HOSKINS, W.G. The making of the English landscape. Harmondsworth, Penguin, 1970.

HOWKINS, Alun. Reshaping rural England: a social history 1850-1925. London, Routledge, 1991.

HUNTER, John. The Essex landscape: a study of its form and history. Chelmsford, Essex Record Office, 1999.

KELLY's Essex directory, 1855-1929.

MINGAY, G.E. Land and society in England 1750-1980. London, Longman, 1994

Nazeing Parish Magazine and Nazeing Parish News.

OGBORNE, Elizabeth. The history of Essex from the earliest time to the present day. London, Longman, 1814.

PRACY, David. Not a better set in the country: the story of Nazeing Wood or Park 1778-1950. Nazeing Conservation Society, 1995.

PRACY, David. Palmer of Nazing: the growth and decline of a west Essex gentry estate 1770-1950. Unpublished University of Essex dissertation, 1998.

RACKHAM, Oliver. The history of the countryside. J. M. Dent 1986.

RANSFORD, Rosalind (ed.) The early charters of the Augustinian canons of Waltham Abbey. Boydell, 1989.

READ, David. The history of All Saints parish church. The church, 1964.

REANEY, P.H. The origin of English place names. London, Routledge & Kegan Paul, 1964.

REANEY, P.H. The place-names of Essex. Cambridge UP, 1969.

RICHARDSON, John. The local historian's encyclopedia., 2nd ed. New Barnet, Historical Publications, 1986.

RICKWORD, Gerald O. A brief summary of the West Essex Yeomanry Cavalry 1830-77. In *Essex Review*, vol.57, 1948.

SELBORNE, 1st Earl (Roundell Palmer). Memorials. London, Macmillan, 1896.

STEVENS, J.S. John Eliot and the Nasing Puritans of the 17th century. Cheshunt, T. Buck, 1874.

STONE, L. and STONE, J.C.F. An open elite? England 1540-1880. Oxford, 1984.

SUTHERLAND, J.R. The history of Nazeing. The author, 1950.

THOMPSON, E.P. Customs in common. Harmondsworth, Penguin, 1993.

VICTORIA County History of Essex, vols. 2, 5, 8.

WHITE's Essex directory, 1848, 1863.

WINTERS, William. Memorials of the Pilgrim Fathers. Waltham Abbey, 1882.

WRIGHT, Thomas. The history and topography of the county of Essex, 1831.

YOUNG, Arthur. General view of the agriculture of Essex. London, Phillips, 1807.

ARCHIVAL SOURCES

Essex Record Office

D/CT 249. Nazeing Tithe Award, 1847

D/DJg B30. Palmer v Guadagni, 1907.

D/DJg B105. Dinah Standingford v George Palmer, 1838. Andrews v George Palmer junior, 1849.

D/DJg M37. Steward's papers, 1637-8.

D/P321. Vestry minutes, rates, church wardens' and overseers' accounts

D/DPm. Palmer estate papers, 1565-1870.

D/DYc. Papers of the Bury family.

Q/RP1. Land tax records.

Q/RPc. Electoral registers.

Q/SR. Typed transcripts of Quarter Sessions records 1570-1711.

T/A 778. Visitation replies to queries relating to the diocese of London, 1790, 1810.

T/B 95. George Palmer's day-book, 1793-1819

T/P 140. WINTERS, William. The history of Nazeing, 1872. Unpublished ms.

T/P 153. WINTERS, William. The history of Warlies, 1891. Unpublished ms.

T/P 181/8/1-19. CUTTLE collection of newspaper cuttings, 1894-1936.

Guildhall Library - Pamphlets and articles related to George Palmer junior and Epping Forest.

Lambeth Palace Library - Selborne papers, for Palmer family documents and letters.

Northamptonshire Record Office - Wake Courteenhall documents.

Public Record Office - Census returns for Nazeing, 1841-91.

Private documents

NAZEING WOOD OR PARK minutes, 1778-1950.

NAZEING PARISH COUNCIL, minutes 1894-1920.

1824 parish survey. Nazeing Parish Council has recently had copies made for display in the village and deposited the original at ERO.

Transcriptions of various other private documents are available from Nazeing History Workshop, subject to the permission of the individual owners.

Reminiscences - Interviews with Enid and Peter Brent, Neville Cole, John Graham, Arthur Hollow, Adelaide Starling.

INDEX